First World War
and Army of Occupation
War Diary
France, Belgium and Germany

14 DIVISION
Divisional Troops
Divisional Cyclist Company
1 July 1915 - 11 May 1916

WO95/1886/2

The Naval & Military Press Ltd
www.nmarchive.com
Published in association with The National Archives

Published by

The Naval & Military Press Ltd

Unit 10 Ridgewood Industrial Park,

Uckfield, East Sussex,

TN22 5QE England

Tel: +44 (0) 1825 749494

www.naval-military-press.com

www.nmarchive.com

This diary has been reprinted in facsimile from the original. Any imperfections are inevitably reproduced and the quality may fall short of modern type and cartographic standards.

© Crown Copyright
Images reproduced by permission of The National Archives, London, England, 2015.

Contents

Document type	Place/Title	Date From	Date To
Heading	1886/2 14th Divisional Cyclist Company		
Heading	14th Division 14th Divl Cyclist Coy. 1915-May 1916		
Miscellaneous	From O.C. 6th Cyclist Battn.	23/05/1916	23/05/1916
Heading	14th Division 14th Divl Cyclist Coy Vol I 7-30.5.15 May 1915 May 1916		
War Diary	Aldershot	07/05/1916	19/05/1916
War Diary	Farnborough	19/05/1916	19/05/1916
War Diary	Southampton	19/05/1916	19/05/1916
War Diary	Harve	20/05/1916	20/05/1916
War Diary	Bavinchove	21/05/1916	21/05/1916
War Diary	Hellesbroucq	21/05/1916	27/05/1916
War Diary	Broxeele	28/05/1916	28/05/1916
War Diary	Steenvoorde	29/05/1916	30/05/1916
Miscellaneous	A Form. Messages And Signals.		
Heading	14th Divisional Cyclist Company Vol. II 31 5-30.6.15		
War Diary	Reninghelst	31/05/1916	12/06/1916
War Diary	S W Of Westoutre	12/06/1916	14/06/1916
War Diary	Watou	15/06/1916	20/06/1916
War Diary	Hilhoek	20/06/1916	30/06/1916
Heading	14th Divisional Cyclist Coy. Vol. III 1-31.7.15		
Heading	War Diary Of 14th Divisional Cyclist Coy. From July 1st To July 31st 1915 (Volume 3)		
War Diary	Hilhoek	01/07/1915	29/07/1915
War Diary	Watou	30/07/1915	31/07/1915
Heading	14th Divisional Cycl. Coy. Vol. IV From 1-31.8.15		
War Diary	Watou	01/08/1915	31/08/1915
Heading	14th Divl Cyclist Coy. Vol. V Sept 15		
Heading	War Diary Of 14th Divisional Cyclist Coy. From September 1st To September 30th 1915 (Volume 5)		
War Diary	Watou	01/09/1915	30/09/1915
Heading	14th Divl Cyclist Coy. Vol 6 Oct 15		
Heading	War Diary Of 14th Divisional Cyclist Coy From October 1st To October 31st 1915 (Volume 6)		
War Diary	Watou	01/10/1915	31/10/1915
Heading	14th Div. Cycl. Coy. Vol. 7 Nov. 15		
Heading	War Diary Of 14th Divisional Cyclist Coy From November 1st To November 30th 1915 (Volume 7)		
Miscellaneous	From O.C. 14th Divisional Cyclist Coy		
War Diary	Watou	01/11/1915	30/11/1915
Miscellaneous	The Officer Commanding, 14th Divisional Cyclist Company.	29/10/1915	29/10/1915
Miscellaneous	From, O.C. 14th Divisional Cyclist Company To Col. i/c A.C.C. Records November.	07/11/1915	07/11/1915
Miscellaneous	14th Co		
Heading	War Diary Of 14th Divisional Cyclist Coy. From Dec 1st To Dec 31st 1915 (Volume 8)		
War Diary	Watou	01/12/1915	31/12/1915
Heading	14th Divl Cyclist Vol 9 Jan 16		
Heading	War Diary Of 14th Divisional Cyclist Coy. From January 1st To January 31st 1916 (Volume 9)		

War Diary	Ste Sixte	01/01/1916	31/01/1916
Heading	War Diary Of 14th Divisional Cyclist Coy. From Feby 1st 1916 To Feby 29th 1916 (Volume 10)		
War Diary	Ste Sixte	01/02/1916	12/02/1916
War Diary	Esquelbecq	13/02/1916	20/02/1916
War Diary	Amiens	20/02/1916	20/02/1916
War Diary	Villers Bocage	21/02/1916	24/02/1916
War Diary	Gezaincourt	25/02/1916	25/02/1916
War Diary	Sus St Leger	25/02/1916	28/02/1916
War Diary	Barly	29/02/1916	29/02/1916
Heading	War Diary Of 14th Divisional Cyclist Coy. From March 1st To March 31st 1916 (Volume 11)		
War Diary	Barly	01/03/1916	19/03/1916
War Diary	Fosseux	19/03/1916	31/03/1916
Heading	War Diary Of 14th Divisional Cyclist Coy. From April 1st To April 30th 1916 (Volume 12)		
War Diary	Fosseux	01/04/1916	29/04/1916
Heading	War Diary Of 14th Divisional Cyclist Coy. From May 1st To May 11th 1916 (Volume 13)		
War Diary	Fosseux	01/05/1916	05/05/1916
War Diary	Izel-Lez-Hameau	06/05/1916	11/05/1916
Heading	14th Div. Cyclist Vol 8		
Miscellaneous	14th Divisional Cyclist Coy.	19/12/1915	19/12/1915
Miscellaneous	14th Divisional Cyclist Coy.		

1886/2
14th Dunavon Cyclist Company

14TH DIVISION

14TH DIVL CYCLIST COY.
MAY 1915 – MAY 1916

THIS FOLDER ALSO CONTAINS
PART OF THE WAR DIARY OF THE
46TH BRIGADE RFA FOR 1915-1916

From O.C.
    6th Cyclist Batt."

To. Officer
   i/c A.G's Office
          Base.

         Herewith War Diary
of 14th Divisional Cyclist Coy to date
of formation of this Battalion.

                    S.P.H.Gurner. Lieut & Adjt
                         6th Cyclist Batt"

VI ~~CORPS~~
CYCLIST BATTALION.
No. 10
Date 23/5/16.

121/5445

14th Division

14th Div¹ Cyclist Coy

Vol 1. 7 — 30. 5? 15.

May 1515
May 1916

May 15

Army Form C. 2118.

WAR DIARY
or
INTELLIGENCE SUMMARY.
(Erase heading not required.)

Instructions regarding War Diaries and Intelligence Summaries are contained in F. S. Regs., Part II. and the Staff Manual respectively. Title pages will be prepared in manuscript.

Place	Date	Hour	Summary of Events and Information	Remarks and references to Appendices
ALDERSHOT	7th	11 p.m	Orders received to close Clothing & Equipment Ledgers on 11th inst.	
"	8th	6 p.m	Surplus Stores of Past Reserve Clothing returned to Field Depot	
"	9th		Mobilizing	
"	10th	12 noon	Orders for Entrainment of Unit received for 15th inst	
"	11th	11.30 a.m	Orders for Entrainment cancelled and amended to read 19th inst, Clothing and Equipment Ledgers closed	
"	12th		Mobilizing	
"	13th		ditto	
"	14th	10 a.m	Local Auditor inspects Clothing & Equipment Ledgers	
"	15th		Mobilizing	
"	16th		ditto	
"	17th	3.30 p.m	Called on Officer i/c Barracks Wellington Lines to arrange about Marching Out Inspection of Barracks.	
"	"	11.30 p.m	Message confirming date of Entrainment for 19th inst received also time Table.	
"	18	9 p.m	Pay & Mess Book closed for forwarding to Regt Paymaster HOUNSLOW by O.C. Details.	

Army Form C. 2118.

WAR DIARY
or
INTELLIGENCE SUMMARY.
(Erase heading not required.)

Instructions regarding War Diaries and Intelligence Summaries are contained in F. S. Regs., Part II. and the Staff Manual respectively. Title pages will be prepared in manuscript.

Place	Date	Hour	Summary of Events and Information	Remarks and references to Appendices
ALDERSHOT	19th	3.a.m	Unit marched out of BADAJOS BARRACKS ALDERSHOT	
FARNBOROUGH	"	4.50am	Unit Entrained at FARNBOROUGH STATION with H.Q. & T.S. 14th Div. R.E. O.C. 14th R.E. appointed O.C. Train.	
SOUTHAMPTON	"	6.30am	arrival at SOUTHAMPTON DOCKS.	
"	"	5 p.m	2 Officers (Vipont, Hare & Skyphn) and 5 men with Baggage Waggons and cycles embarked on S.S COURTFIELD for HARVE.	
"	"	7 p.m	Remainder of Officers (6) with 190 men and 1 men attached from the N.Z. Q.to 14th Div. R.E. embarked on S.S. MONAS QUEEN for HARVE.	
HARVE	20th	8 a.m	Officers and men as above dis-embarked from MONAS QUEEN at HARVE	
"	"	4.30pm	Officers and 5 men with Baggage Waggons and cycles disembarked from COURTFIELD.	
"	"	4.55pm	Unit arrived at HALLE (3) and left for En-training Station at 6.10 pm	
"	"	6.30pm	Unit En-trained at POINT I. GARE DE MARCHANDISES with H. 2rs 42nd Inf. Bde. 14th Signal Coy and 10 100 Bay A.S.C.	
"	"	10.30pm	Train departed — O.C. 14th Div.t bycylist Coy appointed O.C. Train.	
BAVINCHOVE	21st	6.15pm	arrival of train at BAVINCHOVE orders received for Unit to march via WATTEN and GANSPETTE to billets at HELLESBROUCQ	

WAR DIARY
or
INTELLIGENCE SUMMARY.
(Erase heading not required.)

Army Form C. 2118.

Place	Date	Hour	Summary of Events and Information	Remarks and references to Appendices
BAVINCHOVE	21st	8.45pm	Unit left BAVINCHOVE	XV
HELLESBROUCQ	21st	11.55pm	Arrived at billets in HELLESBROUCQ after reporting at H.Q. 2nd Div. Troops Area as ordered.	XV / XVI
"	22nd		Day given up to internal arrangements.	XV
"	23rd	12 noon	Open Air Church Parade	XV / XVI
"	24th	9.30 am	Route march via GANSPETTE - FORET D'EPILECQUES Village of EPEPLIQUES	XVI
"	25th		Route march via HOULLE - MOULLE TILQUES to SALPERWICK; returned via SERQUES - EPERLECQUES to billets for training purposes with permission of G.O.C. 1st Div. Troops Area.	XVI
"	26th	10 am	Pay	XVI
"	27th	10 am	Saw trainers and decided amount due for Billets	XVI / XVII
"		1.10pm	Marched via WATTEN, WULVERDINGHE - VOLKERINCKHOVE to billets at BROXEELE arrived at 3.30pm.	XVI
BROXEELE	28th	7.30 am	Saw trainers and decided amount due for Billets.	XVI / XVII
"	"	7.55 am	Marched via BALEMBERG - CASSEL to billets at STEENVOORDE arriving at 10.45 a.m.	XVI / XVII

Army Form C. 2118.

WAR DIARY
or
INTELLIGENCE SUMMARY.
(Erase heading not required.)

Place	Date	Hour	Summary of Events and Information	Remarks and references to Appendices
STEENVOORDE	29	10.30am	Orders received for Company to proceed to join 5th Bde Cyclists as per message (S/39)	M.1
"	30th	6 a.m.	Marched via ABEELE - HEKSKEN to RENINGHELST arriving at 8.15 a.m.	M.2

"A" Form.   Army Form C. 2121.

MESSAGES AND SIGNALS.   No. of Message

Prefix	Code		Words	Charge	This message is on a/c of:	Recd. at	m.
Office of Origin and Service Instructions.			Sent			Date	
			At	m.	Service.	From	
			To			By	
			By		(Signature of "Franking Officer.")		

TO — 14ᵗʰ Cyclist Company

Sender's Number	Day of Month	In reply to Number	AAA
G 139	29ᵗʰ		

Your company will proceed tomorrow to RENINGHELST moving so as to arrive there at 8 am via ABEELE-HEKSKEN for purpose of being attached to corresponding unit of 5ᵗʰ Division AAA A billeting party of one officer and one NCO will be required to proceed this afternoon reporting at 3 pm to Administrative Offices 5ᵗʰ Division RENINGHELST AAA acknowledge

From 14ᵗʰ Divⁿ.
Place
Time 10·40 am

14th Division.

14th The Divisional Cyclist Company.

Vol: II. 31.5. —— 30.6.15.

121/5885

Army Form C. 2118.

WAR DIARY
or
INTELLIGENCE SUMMARY.
(Erase heading not required.)

14th Division Cyclist Coy

Place	Date	Hour	Summary of Events and Information	Remarks and references to Appendices
RENINGHELST	MAY 31st	9.30 a.p	Officers rode into YPRES with O.E. 5th Divl Cyclists for instructional purposes returning at 2 p.m.	AN
"		5 p.m	O.E. & 2 Officers with O.E. 5th Divl Cyclists proceeded to ZILLEBEKE in order to guide to Officers 7th K.R.S.L.I. to support trenches being constructed there, as the K.R.S.L.I. were acting as relief, these Officers never went in order to point out to their Company Commanders their tasks, the Officers of 14th Divl Cyclist returned at 9.40 p.m.	AN
"		5.45 p.m	1 Sgt, 3 Cpls, & 7 men with party of 5th Divl Cyclists proceeded to ZILLEBEKE for purpose of carrying Barbed wire to Support trench returning at 12.30 a.m	AN
"	June 1st	5.30	2 Officers & 60 R.C.O's then with party of 5th Divl Cyclists proceeded to ZILLEBEKE for purpose of carrying sandbags & barbed wire to support trench returning 1.50 a.m	AN
"	"		3 Officers proceeded with O.E. 5th Cyclists for purpose of guiding Officers of 5th K.S.L.I. to their new tasks at ZILLEBEKE returning at 10.15 p.m	AN

WAR DIARY
or
INTELLIGENCE SUMMARY.
(Erase heading not required.)

Army Form C. 2118.

Place	Date	Hour	Summary of Events and Information	Remarks and references to Appendices
RENINGHELST	2nd	10.30am	O.C & 6 Officers proceeded to BAILLEUL to visit their Comrades returning about 3.30 p.m.	XVI
			1 Officer took the boy to the Baths at RENINGHELST	XVI
		5.45pm	O.C & 2 Officers with 60 N.C.O's then proceeded to ZILLEBEKE for purpose of carrying barbed wire & sand bags to support trenches returning at 3 a.m.	XVI
	3rd	5.45pm	3 Officers & 60 N.C.O's then proceeded to ZILLEBEKE for purpose of carrying barbed wire & sand bags to support trenches returning at 2.30 a.m.	XVI
	4th	7.30pm	2 Officers + 60 N.C.O's then proceeded to ZILLEBEKE for purpose of widening & improving & continuing communication trench. returning at 3 a.m.	XVI
	5th	7.30pm	O.C & 2 Officers + 70 N.C.O then proceeded to ZILLEBEKE for purpose of widening improving & continuing communication trench returning at 3.30 a.m.	XVI
	6th	5.45pm	1 Sgt + 20 men with 5th Aust Cyclists proceeded to ZILLEBEKE with carrying Planks to support trenches returning 12 Midnight	XVI

Army Form C. 2118.

WAR DIARY
or
INTELLIGENCE SUMMARY.
(Erase heading not required.)

Instructions regarding War Diaries and Intelligence Summaries are contained in F. S. Regs., Part II. and the Staff Manual respectively. Title pages will be prepared in manuscript.

Place	Date	Hour	Summary of Events and Information	Remarks and references to Appendices
RENING HELST	6th	7 pm	2 Officers & 49 N.C.O. then proceeded to ZILLEBEKE for purpose of digging trenches returning at 3 a.m.	XI
"	"	11.30 a.m	Church Parade. Senior Chaplin preached (5th Division)	XI
"	7th	7 pm	1 Officer & 5 N.C.O. then proceeded to ZILLEBEKE for purpose of digging trenches returning at 3 a.m.	XI
"	8th	7 pm	2 Officers & 80 N.C.O. then proceeded to ZILLEBEKE for purpose of digging trenches returning at 3.45 a.m.	XI
"	9th	9 a.m	Received orders to move into new Billets at RENINGHELST. Unit received orders to apply to CRE 5th Div for supply of Technology unit 5th Division	XII
"	9th	5 pm	Company proceeded to Billets after Bathing Parade.	XII
"	10	9 a.m	Company at work improving billets etc	XII
"	11th		Heavy fall of rain during night 10th/11th.	
"	11th	5.45 pm	2 Officers & 60 N.C.O. then proceeded to the neighbourhood of BOIS-CARRÉ for purpose of digging trenches returning at 3.30 a.m. 2/Lt Baumgartner wounded in stomach whilst returning from trenches. S/Lt Shepherd accompanied him to hospital at BAILLEUL returning at 7 a.m.	XII
"	12th	12.30 pm	Company moved into new Billets S.W. of WESTOUTRE	XII

WAR DIARY
or
INTELLIGENCE SUMMARY.

Army Form C. 2118.

Place	Date	Hour	Summary of Events and Information	Remarks and references to Appendices
S.W. of WESTOUTRE	12	5.45pm	O.C. & 2 Officers with 100 N.C.O's then proceeded to the neighbourhood of BOISCARRÉ for purpose of digging trenches returning at 4 a.m.	
"	13th	12.15pm	Church Parade under Senior Chaplain 14th Division	
"	14th	8 a.m	Saw Maire and devised amount due for billets	
"		6 a.m	Company proceeded via BOESCHEPE & ABEELE to W. of POPERINGHE to new billets in accordance with operation orders received at 2 a.m.	
POPERINGHE WATOU	15th	10 a.m	Company Inspection and fatigue work	
do	16th	"	ditto ditto	
do	17th	"	ditto ditto	
do	do	10.30 am	Route March by Platoons for Map reading	
do	18th	11.45 am	Interpreter with 2 offrs of this Unit under instructions of Aeroplane re ditto	
do	19	10.30 a.m	ditto ditto	
do		10 a.m	Company Inspection. Route march by Platoons for map reading instruction.	
do		4.30pm	Orders received to move into new billets	
do	20	8.30 a.m	Moved into new billets vacated by 144th Field Ambulance	

Army Form C. 2118.

WAR DIARY
or
INTELLIGENCE SUMMARY.
(Erase heading not required.)

Instructions regarding War Diaries and Intelligence Summaries are contained in F. S. Regs, Part II. and the Staff Manual respectively. Title pages will be prepared in manuscript.

Place	Date	Hour	Summary of Events and Information	Remarks and references to Appendices
DICKEBUSCH HUTS HILL HOEK	20th	12 midnight	1 Corpl & 5 men left for purpose of guiding 43rd Field Ambulance to billets vacated by this Unit, returning at 4.30 a.m.	
ditto	21st	7 a.m	Physical Exercise	
"	"	10 a.m	Company Inspection. Route march by Platoons for trumpeting instruction	
"	"	3.30 pm	Company Pay	
"	22nd	7 a.m	Physical Exercise	
"	"	10 a.m	Company Inspection. Route march by Platoons for map reading instruction	
"	23rd	7 a.m	Physical Exercise	
"	"	9.30 a.m	6 men left to report to 14th Signal Coy for duty as Despatch Riders	
"	"	10 a.m	Company Inspection & maps drawing	
"	24th	7 a.m	Physical Exercise	
"	"	9 a.m	4 N.C.O.s & 8 men left for purpose of reporting to 14th Division for duty as Military Police.	
"	"	10 a.m	Gen Kit inspection by C.O.	
"	"	11 p.m	2nd in command & 16 men proceeded to join Billeting Parties of 42nd Brigade, in order to acquaint them to send guides to meet approaching Battalions for purpose of leading them to their station Billets as per instructions received at 16.30 p.m by message from G.S.O. 14th Division	

Army Form C. 2118.

WAR DIARY
or
INTELLIGENCE SUMMARY.
(Erase heading not required.)

Instructions regarding War Diaries and Intelligence Summaries are contained in F. S. Regs., Part II. and the Staff Manual respectively. Title pages will be prepared in manuscript.

Place	Date	Hour	Summary of Events and Information	Remarks and references to Appendices
HILHOEK	25th	7a.m.	Physical Exercises	XV
"	"	10a.m.	Company Inspection and map reading. Platoon Commanders & N.C.O's left to find out whereabouts of different units in Resting Area.	XV
"	26th	10a.m.	Company Inspection, O.C. & 4 Officers proceeded through YPRES for reconnaissance work	XV
"	"	2.30pm	Route March	
"	27th	10.45am	Church Parade	XV
"	"	6.30pm	1 Officer & 50 N.C.O's & men proceeded through YPRES for purpose of digging trenches returning at 3.30 a.m.	XV
"	"		1 Officer & 19 N.C.O's & men proceeded through YPRES for purpose of salvage work	
"	28th	6.30pm	2 Officers & 70 N.C.O's & men proceeded through YPRES for purpose of digging trenches returning at 3.30 a.m.	XV
"	29th	"	1 Officer & 50 N.C.O's & men proceeded through YPRES for purpose of digging trenches returning at 3 a.m.	XV
"	"	"	Salvage party returned at 3. a. m	

1577 Wt.W10791/1773 500,000 1/15 D.D.&L. A.D.S.S./Forms/C. 2118.

WAR DIARY
or
INTELLIGENCE SUMMARY.

Place	Date	Hour	Summary of Events and Information	Remarks and references to Appendices
HILHOEK	30th	6.30pm	10 Officers + 50 N.C.O.s/men proceeded to YPRES for purpose of carrying Bombs, returning at 3 a.m.	XV

14th Division.

181/6250

14th Divisional Cyclist Coy.
Vol. III 1 — 31.7.15.

Confidential

War Diary.

of

14th Divisional Cyclist Coy.

from July 1st to July 31st 1915

(Volume 3)

Army Form C. 2118.

WAR DIARY
or
INTELLIGENCE SUMMARY.
(Erase heading not required.)

Instructions regarding War Diaries and Intelligence Summaries are contained in F.S. Regs., Part II. and the Staff Manual respectively. Title pages will be prepared in manuscript.

Place	Date	Hour	Summary of Events and Information	Remarks and references to Appendices
HILHOEK	July 1	6.30pm	1 Officer (2/Lt a.f. from) & 20 men proceeded through YPRES for purpose of Salvage work. Report of work done forwarded to Div HQt 2/Lt on 1st inst	XII
"	2nd	12 noon	Company Inspection.	XII
"	"	9pm	Salvage Party Returned; Report on work done forwarded to Div Hd Qts on 4th inst	XII
"	3rd	10.14.a.m	Cpl ——— 1st NCO then proceeded to POPERINGHE to report to Town Major for duty.	XII
"	4th	10 wan	Church parade	XI
"	"	6.30pm	1 Officer (2/Lt S.Skynner) 50 N.C.O & men proceeded through YPRES for purpose of trench digging	XII
"	5th	3 pm	Company Pay.	XI
"	6th	12 noon	Company Inspection.	XII
"	"	6.30pm	1 Officer (Lt Horwitz) 50 NCOs & men proceeded through YPRES for purpose of trench digging	XII
"	7th	12 noon	Company Inspection	XI
"	8th	"	(2/Lt Pakenham) ditto	XII
"	"	6.30pm	1 Officer & 50 NCO & men proceeded through YPRES for purpose of trench digging.	XII

Army Form C. 2118.

WAR DIARY
or
INTELLIGENCE SUMMARY.
(Erase heading not required.)

Instructions regarding War Diaries and Intelligence Summaries are contained in F. S. Regs., Part II. and the Staff Manual respectively. Title pages will be prepared in manuscript.

Place	Date	Hour	Summary of Events and Information	Remarks and references to Appendices
HILHOEK.	9th	9 a.m.	Company proceeded to POPERINGHE to Divisional Baths.	W.J.
"	"	12 a.m.	Company Lecture (2nd Lt. B.I. Williams)	W.J.
"	"	4.30 p.m.	Officer & 21 N.C.O's then proceeded to firing line beyond YPRES for salvage work.	W.J.
"	10th	12 a.m.	Company Parade	W.J.
"	11th	9.15 a.m.	Church Parade	W.J.
"	12th	12 a.m.	Company Parade (2nd Lt. M.A. Burton)	W.J.
"	"	4.30 p.m.	1 Officer 21 N.C.O then proceeded to firing line beyond YPRES for salvage work.	W.J.
"	"	6 p.m.	(2nd Lt. S.R. Gunn) 1 Officer 80 men proceeded through YPRES for purpose of digging 4 Brit Half Coln on 13 inst	W.J.
"	"	9.30 p.m.	Salvage party returned. Report on work above reported to 14 Bgd Half Coln on 13 inst	W.J.
"	13th	12 a.m.	Company Parade. Heavy rain fell during night 13th/14th	W.J.
"	14th	"	ditto	W.J.
"	15th	"	ditto	W.J.
"	16th	"	ditto	W.J.
"	"	4 p.m.	2/Lt S.R. Gunn & 21 N.C.O's then proceeded to firing line for salvage work.	W.J.

WAR DIARY
or
INTELLIGENCE SUMMARY.

Army Form C. 2118.

Place	Date	Hour	Summary of Events and Information	Remarks and references to Appendices
HILHOEK	16th	7 p.m.	1 Sgt + 9 men proceeded to firing line to join Salvage Party.	[initials]
"	"	9.30 p.m.	2/Lt Harbutson's salvage party returned. Report forwarded to H.Q. 4th Bde re 17 insp. Heavy rain fell during night 16/17	[initials]
"	17th	12 n.	Company Parade	[initials]
"	18th	9.30 a.m.	Church Parade	[initials]
"	19th	12 n.	Company Parade & Pay Parade	[initials]
"	"	2.30 p.m.	1 Officer (2 Lt A.S. Howe) + 30 men proceeded to firing line for purpose of Salvage Work.	[initials]
"	"	6.30 p.m.	7th A.M.K. Summers's Salvage Party returned.	[initials]
"	20th	12 n.	Company Parade	[initials]
"	"	6 p.m.	1 Officer (2/Lt S.P. Shepherd) + 40 men proceeded through YPRES for purpose of arranging skinning at 12.30 p.m. work prevented owing to bombardment.	[initials]
"	21st	12 n.	Company Parade. O.C. & Lt Harrison proceeded to firing line Transport Staff (Salvage) also visiting personnel of Brigade Headquarters returning at 8 p.m.	[initials]
"	"		for purpose of arranging skinning returning at 8 p.m.	[initials]
"	22nd	11 a.m.	O.C. proceeded through YPRES for reconnaissance work in new line of trenches taken over by 14th Division for G.O.C. Division returning at 8 p.m.	[initials]

WAR DIARY or INTELLIGENCE SUMMARY.

Army Form C. 2118.

Place	Date	Hour	Summary of Events and Information	Remarks and references to Appendices
HILHOEK	22nd	12 noon	Company Parade	XI
"	"	6 p.m.	2 Parties (2d Harrison & 74 Clephorn) 40 Men proceeded through YPRES for purpose of building a redoubt returning at 3 a.m. Heavy rain fell during night 22nd/23rd.	XII
"	23rd	12 noon	Company Parade	XIII
"	"	9.30 p.m.	2/Lt Athore Salvage Party returned, reports on work done forwarded on 23rd inst.	XIV
"	24th	12 noon	Company Parade	XV
"	25th	9.30 a.m.	Church Parade (2 battalion)	XV
"	"	6 p.m.	O.C. & 10 Officers & 50 Men proceeded through YPRES for purpose of building Machine Gun emplacement, Motor Buses were supplied by the Division to carry the party to YPRES by recently into hut billets at WATOU	XVI
"	26th	12 noon	Company moved into hut billets at WATOU by motor Buses	XVI
"	27th	7 p.m.	2 Officers (2/Lt Evans's & 2/Lt Wilson's) + 48 Men proceeded through YPRES for purpose of building Machine Gun emplacement	XVII
"	28th	12 noon	Company Parade	XVIII
"	29th	11 a.m.	Company Parade & Inspection of Kits	
"	10th Sat		O.C. proceeded through YPRES for reconnaissance work in new line of trenches taken over by 14 Division for G.O.C. returning at 6 p.m.	XIX

Army Form C. 2118.

WAR DIARY
or
INTELLIGENCE SUMMARY.
(Erase heading not required.)

Place	Date	Hour	Summary of Events and Information	Remarks and references to Appendices
WATOU	30th	4.30pm	2/Bedfordshire & 30 MC on their proceed to firing line for salvage work	W.J. H.J.
"	31	12 noon	Company Parade.	

121/6607

14th Division

14th Divisional Cycl: Coy:
Vol: IX
From 1 - 3 - 6. 15

WAR DIARY or INTELLIGENCE SUMMARY

Army Form C. 2118.

14 Div: Cyclist Coy

Place	Date	Hour	Summary of Events and Information	Remarks and references to Appendices
WATOU	Aug 1st	8.30 a.m.	Church Parade.	
"	2nd	6 p.m.	1 Officer (2Lt Shepherd) + 30 men proceeded to YPRES for purpose of filling in a cable trench.	XIV
"	3rd	8.30 p.m.	Salvage Party returned.	XV
"	"	6 p.m.	1 Officer (Lt H.S. Harrison) + 50 men proceeded through YPRES for purpose of digging. O.C. at request of Divisional Staff proceeded to the trenches + made a reconnaissance with a view to making an attack in order to regain the trenches lost in the German attack of 30th & 31st July.	XVI
"	4th	"	1 Officer (2Lt Arthur) + 30 men proceeded through YPRES for purpose of digging.	XVII
"	5th	"	1 Officer (2Lt S.R. Rickman) + 50 men proceeded through YPRES for purpose of digging. O.C. at request of Divisional Staff made a reconnaissance of the G.H.Q. trench in order to make a permanent enlarged Staff Map for use during its reconstruction.	XVIII
"	6th	"	1 Officer (2Lt Masterton) + 50 men proceeded through YPRES for purpose of digging. O.C. commenced enlargement of G.H.Q. trench to scale 2500 for Division.	XIX
"	"	4.30 p.m.	2Lt Arthur + 30 men proceeded to join him for salvage work.	XX
"	7th	6 p.m.	1 Officer (Lt H.S. Harrison) + 50 men proceeded through YPRES for purpose of carrying. O.C. finished enlarged Sketch Map on linen for Divisional Staff.	XXI
"	"	6.15 p.m.	1 Officer (2Lt Shepherd) + 30 men proceeded through YPRES for purpose of digging.	XXII

WAR DIARY
or
INTELLIGENCE SUMMARY.
(Erase heading not required.)

Army Form C. 2118.

Place	Date	Hour	Summary of Events and Information	Remarks and references to Appendices
WATOU	8th	7a.m.	Sketch map forwarded to Divl Headquarters also Report on condition of G.H.Q Trench 2.A. Eames saw Mann ref Rebilling Certificate	XV
"	9th	12 noon	Company Inspection	XV
"	"	2.30 pm	10 Officers (Pte S. Shephard) & 30 men proceeded to firing line for Salvage work	XVI XVI
"	10th	6.30 pm	2 Lt Williams Salvage Party returned	XVI
"	"	12 noon	Company Inspection	XVI
"	11th		G.H.Q. Trench.	XVI
"	"	6.30am	O.C. & 2nd in Command proceeded to Headquarters preparatory of completing reconnaissance	XVI
"	"	6 pm	N.C.O.	XVI
"	"		2nd Lt Shepherd & 15 men (Sgt Robertson) proceeded through YPRES for purpose of carrying reconnaissance. Also Party	
"	12th	10.30 pm	2nd Lt Shepherd's Salvage Party returned, relieved by 14th Div L Cavalry.	
"	13th	12 noon	Company Parade.	
"	"	"	ditto.	
"	"	8.30 am	O.C. & 2nd in Command proceeded E of VLAMERTINGHE reconnoitring a new Bivouac for the Unit	XV
"	"		AMERTINGHE for purpose to YPRES	
"	"	6.30	1 N.C.O (Sgt Phillips) & 25 men proceeded to DIXMUDE GATE to report to R.E	XV
"	14th	12 noon	Company Parade	XV
"	15th	9.30 am	Church Parade	XV
"	"	6 P.M.	1 N.C.O (4 Sgt Welsey) & 25 men proceeded to DIXMUDE GATE YPRES to report to R.E	XV

WAR DIARY
or
INTELLIGENCE SUMMARY.

Army Form C. 2118.

Place	Date	Hour	Summary of Events and Information	Remarks and references to Appendices
WATOU	16th	2.p.m	2 Lt J.R.K Green + 30 men proceeded to firing line for purpose of Salvage	XI
"	"	4.30 pm	Pay Parade	XI
"	17th	6 p.m	1 N.C.O (Sgt Bowen) & 28 men proceeded to BIRMUDE GATE YPRES but owing to bombardment with gas shells could not get through YPRES so returned at 11 p.m. Pte Morris gassed also two others slightly	XI
"	18th	12 noon	Company Parade	XI
"	19th	6 p.m	1 Officer (2Lt Robertson) + 4 O.N.C.O + men proceeded (by Motor Lorries) through YPRES for purpose of constructing a redoubt.	XI
"	20th	2 p.m	2 Lt A L han + 30 men proceeded to firing line for purpose of Salvage	XI
"	"	6 p.m	2 Lt S.R.A.Grunin's Salvage Party returned	XI
"	21st	6 p.m	2 Lt H.S.Harrison + 60 men proceeded through YPRES for purpose of digging	XI
"	22nd	2 p.m	Church Parade.	XI
"	23rd	2 p.m	2 Lt H.Robertson & 30 men proceeded to firing line for purpose of Salvage	XI
"	"	6 p.m	2 Lt A Man's Salvage Party returned.	XI
"	24th	12 noon	Company Parade	XI

Army Form C. 2118.

WAR DIARY
or
INTELLIGENCE SUMMARY.
(Erase heading not required.)

Place	Date	Hour	Summary of Events and Information	Remarks and references to Appendices
WATOU	25th	12am	Company Parade.	W.J.
"	26th		Company Parade.	W.J.
"	27th	2p	2/Lt Williams + 30 men proceeded to firing-line for purpose of salvage work.	W.J.
"	"	6pm	2/Lt Robertson's party returned. (Sgt Bowen, L/Cpl Skelly + Pte Austin wounded on 25th inst)	W.J.
"	28th	6p.m.	2/Lt Shepherd + 60 men proceeded through YPRES for purpose of digging	W.J.
"	29th	9.15am	Church Parade	W.J.
"	30th	1.30pm	Battery Parade	W.J.
"	"	6pm	2/Lt A.E. Thom + 50 men proceeded through YPRES for purpose of digging	W.J.
"	31st	10.30	Company Parade.	W.J.
"	"	11pm	2/Lt Williams 'Salvage' Party returned.	W.J.

1577 Wt. W10791/1773 500,000 1/15 D. D. & L. A.D.S.S./Forms/C. 2118.

14th Division

14th Div'l Cyclist Coy:
vol: V
Sept. 15

Confidential.

War Diary
of
14th Divisional Cyclist Coy.

from September 1st to September 30th 1915.

(Volume 5)

Army Form C. 2118.

WAR DIARY
or
INTELLIGENCE SUMMARY.
(Erase heading not required.)

Place	Date	Hour	Summary of Events and Information	Remarks and references to Appendices
WATOU	1st	7 a.m	Lieut J.R.K. Brown & 17 men were attached to 6th Army Corps A.P.M. for road control duties.	XIV
"	2nd		Room Company Inspection	XIV
"	3rd		" "	XIV
"	4th		" "	XIV
"	5	10 a.m	Church Parade	
"	6th	3 p.m	2nd Lt O. Williams & 25 men proceeded to report to 4th Cavalry Bde. for purpose of wood-cutting for bivouacs. 2nd Lieut WILLIAMS takes command of 25 men of 14th Divl Cavalry and 2 Sqdn 14th Divl Cyclists; they proceeded by train from POPERINGHE to EBBLINGHEM; cutting to be done in the FORET DE CLAIRMARAIS	XIV
"	7th	2 p.m	Lieut S. SHEPHERD & 12 men proceed to firing line for purpose of Salvage Work.	XIV
"	8	1.30 p	O.C. & 70 men proceeded to YPRES by train from POPERINGHE for purpose of digging cable trench.	XIV
"	9th	3 p.m	Company Parade.	
"	10	2 p.m	Lieut A.L. Mace & 12 men proceed to firing line for purpose of Salvage Work.	XIV

WAR DIARY
or
INTELLIGENCE SUMMARY.
(Erase heading not required.)

Army Form C. 2118.

Place	Date	Hour	Summary of Events and Information	Remarks and references to Appendices
WATOU	10	5pm	Lieut S. Shepherd's Salvage Party returned. O.C. proceeded on leave.	
"	11	12 noon	Company Parade.	
"	12	10 am	Church Parade	
"	13	12 noon	Company Parade	
"	"	2 pm	Lieut. S. Hutchinson & 12 men proceeded to firing line for purpose of Salvage work	
"	"	6 pm	Lieut A. L. Rice's Salvage party returned	
"	14	8 am	Company proceeded to POPERINGHE to quiet Parks.	
"	14	6.30 pm	Lieut S. Shepherd & 60 men proceeded to YPRES by train from POPERINGHE for purpose Salvaging cable hints.	
"	"	8 pm	10 Officers (2/Lt R.F. Youngs) & 21 men joined the Unit from depot.	
"	15	3 pm	Company Parade.	
"	16	12 noon	ditto	
"	"		O.C. returned off leave.	
"	17	2 pm	Lieut. Hutchinson & 2/Lt. R.F. Youngs & 12 men proceeded to firing line for purpose of Salvage Work	
"	"	3.30 pm	Lieut Hutchinson's Salvage Party returned	

WAR DIARY
or
INTELLIGENCE SUMMARY.

Army Form C. 2118.

Place	Date	Hour	Summary of Events and Information	Remarks and references to Appendices
WATOU	18th	12 noon	Company Parade	
"	19th	10 am	Church Parade	
"	20th	12 noon	Company Parade	
"	"	6 pm	Salvage Party returned	
"	21st	5:15 pm	O.C. & 60 men proceed to YPRES by train from POPERINGHE for purpose	
"	22nd	2 pm	Company Parade	
"	23rd	5 pm	Lieut Hotchkison + 70 men proceed to YPRES for purpose of loading unloading waggons	
"	"	3:30	4 men proceed to YPRES	
"	24	4 pm	O.C. & 13 men proceeded through YPRES for purpose of taking charge of a section of the MENIN Rd E of their place, with orders to repairing any holes made by enemies shell fire, & clear the road of any other obstruction likely to impede traffic during operations on the night 24/25th	
"	"		Lieut Hotchkison + 13 men through VLAMERTINGHE to take charge of a section of the road W of YPRES for purpose on above	

Army Form C. 2118.

WAR DIARY
or
INTELLIGENCE SUMMARY.
(Erase heading not required.)

Instructions regarding War Diaries and Intelligence Summaries are contained in F. S. Regs., Part II. and the Staff Manual respectively. Title pages will be prepared in manuscript.

Place	Date	Hour	Summary of Events and Information	Remarks and references to Appendices
WATOU	24th	4.30pm	Lieut H.B.Harrison appointed by G.O.C. 14th Division as Officer to Reconnoitre Party, with Lieut J. Shepherd & 50 men proceeded through YPRES in order to take up his duties during attack on night 24/25th.	IV
"	25th	5.8pm	Lieut S.P.K.Turner + 15 men proceeded to POPERINGHE to act as guard	V
			for prisoners taken during attack night 24/25th	VI
"	26th	4pm	Lieut H.B.Harrison reported the Matthews & J.Shephers wounded	
		7am	Message received from A.P.M. that Repair Parties except the withdrawn	VII
			O.C.'s Party arrived at billets at 10 a.m. Lieut H.B.Harrison's Party arrived	VIII
			at 11 a.m. No damage done to the Sections of the Route to impede the	IX
			Traffic.	X
"	27th	2pm	Lieut H.B.Harrison reported to Lt. T. Jones killed, Pte Armstrong	XI
"	28th	8pm	Lieut H.B.Harrison's Party returned.	XII
"	29th		The Company engaged in clearing the ditches around Camp.	XIII
"	30th	10 a.m.	Heavy Rain fell during the day.	XIV
			Company Rest.	XV

12/7518

14th Kinnaurn

14th Str L. Gecher bn
rd 6
Oct 15

Confidential

War Diary
of
14th Divisional Cyclist Coy

from October 1st to October 31st 1915.

(Volume 6)

Army Form C. 2118.

WAR DIARY
or
INTELLIGENCE SUMMARY.
(Erase heading not required.)

Instructions regarding War Diaries and Intelligence Summaries are contained in F. S. Regs., Part II. and the Staff Manual respectively. Title pages will be prepared in manuscript.

Place	Date	Hour	Summary of Events and Information	Remarks and references to Appendices
WATOU	Oct. 1st	12 noon	Company Parade. Lieut J. Shepherd proceeded on leave.	
"	2nd	"	ditto	
"	3rd	4 p.m.	Lieut A. L. Frere & 50 men proceeded to YPRES for purpose of digging.	
"	4th	12 p.m.	Company Parade; Company proceeded to POPERINGHE for use of 1st Hot Baths.	
"	"	2 p.m.	2/Lieut Blainville & 30 men proceeded to firing line for purpose of salvage work.	
"	5th	12 noon	Company Parade.	
"	6th	"	ditto	
"	"	"	ditto	Lieut M.O. Mauseum proceeded on leave. Lieut Shepherd returned from leave.
"	7th	2 p.m.	Lieut A. L. Frere + 30 men proceeded to firing line for purpose of salvage work.	
"	8th	6 p.m.	2/Lieut J.R. Williams' party returned.	
"	9th	12 noon	Company Parade.	
"	"	"	Lieut J. Shepherd & 15 men reported to A.P.M. 6th Corps for duty on Road Patrols.	
"	10th	10 am	Church Parade.	
"	11th	9 a.m.	Company moved into new billets - the CONVENT, WATOU.	
"	"	2.30 p.m.	2/Lieut M.F. George & 30 men proceeded to firing line for purpose of salvage work.	
"	"	6 p.m.	Lieut A.L. Frere's party returned. 2/Lieut L.B. WILLIAMS proceeded on leave.	

WAR DIARY or INTELLIGENCE SUMMARY

Army Form C. 2118.

(Erase heading not required.)

Instructions regarding War Diaries and Intelligence Summaries are contained in F. S. Regs., Part II. and the Staff Manual respectively. Title pages will be prepared in manuscript.

Place	Date	Hour	Summary of Events and Information	Remarks and references to Appendices
WATOU	Oct 12th	12 p.m.	Company parade	
"	13th	8.30 a.m.	Company proceeded to POPERINGHE for baths. Lieut H.G.Harrison returned from leave	
"	14th	2 p.m.	Company route march	
"	15th	2 p.m.	Lieut H.G.Harrison & 30 men proceeded to firing line for purpose of salvage work.	
"	"	6 p.m.	2/Lieut R.G. Burg's party returned	
"	16th	12 noon	Company parade. Lieut A.R. Emmerson & 6 of 2nd Mtd. Sgt. proceeded on leave	
"	17th	4 p.m.	Church Parade	
"	18th	2 p.m.	Company route march	
"	"	3 p.m.	Lieut H.G.Harrison & salvage party returned.	
"	19th	12 noon	Company parade	
"	20th	10 a.m.	Company ditto	
"	21st	10 a.m.	ditto	
"	22nd	"	ditto	Lieut A.R. Emmerson & 6 of 2nd Mtd. Sgt returned from leave
"	23rd	"	ditto	
"	24th	3.30 p.m.	Church Parade	2/Lieut R.B. William returned from leave

WAR DIARY
or
INTELLIGENCE SUMMARY.
(Erase heading not required.)

Army Form C. 2118.

Place	Date	Hour	Summary of Events and Information	Remarks and references to Appendices
WATOU	Oct			
	25th	3.30pm	Company Pay 1 Cpl Proceed to 2nd Army Grenade School	N.
	26th	10am	Company Drill	N.
			Coy Lt Wayon & 1 Sgt Proceeded on leave	N.
	27th	8.30am	1 NCO and 2 men proceeded to ABEELE for inspection by H.M. the King	N.
		12noon	Company Runs	N.
			Loading Party - 1 NCO and 25 men Proceeded to R.E. dump POPERINGHE	N.
		3.30pm	1 NCO and 5 men returned from course at 1st Division Grenade School	N.
	28th	8am	Loading Party - 1 NCO & 25 men Proceeded to R.E. dump POPERINGHE returning 3.30 p.m	N.
	29th	8am	Loading Party - 1 NCO & 25 men Proceeded to R.E. dump POPERINGHE returning at 3.30 p.m	N.
		10am	Company Route March	N.
	30th	8am	Loading Party - 1 NCO & 25 men Proceeded to R.E. dump POPERINGHE returning at 3.30 p.m	N.
		10am	Company Route March	N.
	31st	3.30pm	Church Parade	N.J.

M. Sh. Gel. Cy.
Vol: 7

12/
7634

Nov. 15

K.

Confidential.

War Diary
of
14th Divisional Cyclist Coy

From November 1st to November 30th 1915.

(Volume 7)

From.
  O.C.
    14th Divisional Cyclist Coy.

To the Officer
  i/c Adjutant General's Office
    Base.

Herewith War Diary of this Unit for November.

M H Towler
  Capt.
COMMANDING
14TH DIVISIONAL CYCLIST COMPANY.

Army Form C. 2118.

WAR DIARY
or
INTELLIGENCE SUMMARY.
(Erase heading not required.)

Instructions regarding War Diaries and Intelligence Summaries are contained in F.S. Regs., Part II. and the Staff Manual respectively. Title pages will be prepared in manuscript.

Place	Date	Hour	Summary of Events and Information	Remarks and references to Appendices
WATOU	1915 NOV 1st	10 a.m.	Company Route March	
"	2nd	12.30 p	Company Parade	
"			Heavy Rain fell	
"	3rd	10 a.m.	Company Route March. 2/Lt Sgt Hayes & 1 A/Sgt returns from leave	
"	4th	12.30 p	Company Parade	
"	5th	10 a.m.	Company Route March	
"	"	"	ditto. Lieut H. Robertson 239% 1 Bpl proceeds on leave	
"	6th	7 a.m.	Working Party 2 R.C.O.s & 40 men proceed to R.E. park POPERINGHE returning at 3.30 pm	
"	"	6 a.m.	ditto	
"	7th	"	Working Party 1 R.C.O & 25 men proceed to 61st Coy R.E. POPERINGHE returning at 4 p.m. Church Parade.	
"	8th	2 p		
"	"	6 a.m.	Working Party 2 R.C.O.s & 40 men proceed to R.E park POPERINGHE returning at 3 pm	
"	"	"	1 R.C.O & 25 men proceed to 61st Coy R.E. POPERINGHE returning at 3 pm	
"	9th	"	ditto	
"	"	"	Working Party 2 R.C.O ated men proceed to R.E. park POPERINGHE returning at 3 pm	

Army Form C. 2118.

WAR DIARY
or
INTELLIGENCE SUMMARY.
(Erase heading not required.)

Instructions regarding War Diaries and Intelligence Summaries are contained in F. S. Regs., Part II. and the Staff Manual respectively. Title pages will be prepared in manuscript.

Place	Date	Hour	Summary of Events and Information	Remarks and references to Appendices
WATOU	10th	8am	Working Party 1 N.C.O. & 25 men proceeded to 61st Coy R.E. POPERINGHE returning at 3pm	
"	"	"	" 2 N.C.O & 40 men proceeded to R.E. Park POPERINGHE returning at 5 p.m.	
"	11th	"	ditto	
"	"	3pm	39 N.C.O & 25 men proceeded to 61st Coy R.E. returning at 3pm	
"	"	2pm	1 N.C.O. & 25 men attended funeral of Belgian Soldier killed in Watou hut burial at WATOU	
"	"	"	Company proceeded to POPERINGHE for use of baths	
"	12th	8am	Working Party 2 N.C.O & 40 men proceeded to R.E. park POPERINGHE returning at 5pm	
"	"	"	" 1 N.C.O & 25 men proceeded to 61st Coy R.E. POPERINGHE " 2pm	
"	13th	"	ditto	
"	"	"	" 2 N.C.O & 40 men proceeded to R.E Park POPERINGHE returning at 3pm	
"	"	"	ditto	
"	14th	2pm	Church Parade	
"	15th	8am	Working Party 2 N.C.O & 40 men proceeded to R.E. Park POPERINGHE returning at 5pm	
"	16th	"	ditto	
"	17th	"	ditto	
"	18th	"	ditto	
"	19th	"	ditto	

WAR DIARY or INTELLIGENCE SUMMARY

Army Form C. 2118.

Place	Date	Hour	Summary of Events and Information	Remarks and references to Appendices
WATOU	20th	8 a.m.	Working Party 2 N.C.O's & 40 men proceeded to R.E. Park POPERINGHE returning at 5 p.m.	AJ.
"		9.30 a.m.	14th Inf. Bde Staff sent car to take LIEUT. A. L. MARE & 2nd Lieut R.F. GWYN to trenches (in front their) where they were taken to observing posts by G.S.O.3 returning at 5.45 p.m.	AJ.
"		3 p.m.	Lieut S.R.K. BURNER & 32 N.C.O's & men proceeded to 14th Inf. Grenade School to attend a course.	AJ.
"	21st	8 a.m.	Working Party 2 N.C.O's & 40 men proceeded to R.E. Park POPERINGHE returning at 5 p.m.	AJ.
"		8.30 a.m.	1 N.C.O & 13 men proceeded to HOUTKERQUE for purpose of loading R.E. material. O.C. & Lieut H.D. HARRISON proceeded to 14th Inf. Grenade School to attend course returning	AJ.
"		4.30 p.m.	they visited the TOWN MAJOR, POPERINGHE in evening by order Maj. *D.* Staff arranging billets for this Unit in POPERINGHE if possible	AJ.
"	22nd	8 a.m.	Working Party 2 N.C.O's & 40 men proceeded to R.E. Park POPERINGHE returning at 5 p.m. and provide 1 N.C.O & 16 men proceeded to VLAMERTINGHE to report at D.A.D.S. 14th Inst Photographic	AJ.
"		12 noon	for purpose of salvage work.	AJ.
"		2 p.m.	Lieut A. L. MARE & 1 man proceeded to trenches to take up position as Intelligence Observation Officer, attached to 43rd Infantry Brigade.	AJ.
"		"	2/Lieut R.F. GWYN & 1 N.C.O ditto, attached to 42nd Inf. Bgde.	AJ.
"		8.30 a.m.	O.C. & Lieut H.D. HARRISON proceeded to 14th Inf. Grenade School to attend course returning at 5 p.m.	AJ.

Army Form C. 2118.

WAR DIARY
or
INTELLIGENCE SUMMARY.
(Erase heading not required.)

Instructions regarding War Diaries and Intelligence Summaries are contained in F. S. Regs., Part II. and the Staff Manual respectively. Title pages will be prepared in manuscript.

Place	Date	Hour	Summary of Events and Information	Remarks and references to Appendices
WATOU	23rd	8 a.m.	Loading Party 2 N.C.O. & 40 men proceeded to R.E. Park POPERINGHE returning at 5 p.m.	XII
"	"	8.30 a.m.	O.C. & Lieut H.D. HARRISON proceeded to 14th Divisional Grenade School to attend course returning about 5 p.m.	XII
"	24th	8 a.m.	Loading Party 2 N.C.O. & 40 men proceeded to R.E. Park POPERINGHE returning at 5 p.m.	XII
"	"	8.30 a.m.	O.C. & Lieut H.D. HARRISON proceeded to 14th Divt Grenade School to attend course returning about 5 p.m.	XII
"	25th	8 a.m.	Loading Party 2 N.C.O. & 40 men proceeded to R.E. Park POPERINGHE returning at 5 p.m.	XII
"	"	8.30 a.m.	O.C. & Lieut H.D. HARRISON proceeded to 14th Divt Grenade School to attend course returning about 5 p.m.	XII
"	26th	8 a.m.	Loading Party 2 N.C.O. & 40 men proceeded to R.E. Park POPERINGHE returning at 5 p.m.	XII
"	"	8.30 a.m.	O.C. & Lieut H.D. HARRISON proceeded to 14th Divt Grenade School to attend course returning about 5 p.m. Slight fall of Snow in morning.	XII
"	27th	8 a.m.	Loading Party 2 N.C.O. O & 140 men proceeded to R.E. Park POPERINGHE returning at 5 p.m.	XII
"	"	8.30 a.m.	O.C. & Lieut H.D. HARRISON proceeded to 14th Divt Grenade School to attend course	XII
"	28th	8 a.m.	Loading Party 2 N.C.O. & 40 men proceeded to R.E. Park POPERINGHE returning at 3 p.m.	XII
"	"	8.30 a.m.	O.C. & Lieut H.D. HARRISON proceeded to 14th Divt Grenade School to attend course returning about 5 p.m.	XII

Army Form C. 2118.

WAR DIARY
or
INTELLIGENCE SUMMARY.
(Erase heading not required.)

Place	Date	Hour	Summary of Events and Information	Remarks and references to Appendices
WATOU	28th	2p.m.	Church Parade.	Nil
"	29th	8am	Working Party 2 N.C.O's & 40 men proceeded to R.E. Park POPERINGHE returning at 5p.m.	Nil
"		8a.m.	O.C. & Lieut H.D. HARRISON proceeded to 14th Bde Grenade School to attend course returning about 6p.m. (Course finished)	Nil
"		6p.m.	Lieut S.R.K. TURNER & 32 N.C.O then returned from 14th Bde Grenade School.	Nil
"	30th	8a.m.	Working Party 2 N.C.O's & 40 men proceeded to R.E. Park POPERINGHE returning at 5p.m.	Nil

E/20139

The Officer Commanding,
14th Divisional Cyclist Company.

        To enable me to comply with para 1930 King's Regulations 1912, please forward the following information:-

(i)   The Date of Formation of Company.

(ii)   Any unusual means by which it was recruited or transfers received.

(iii)   The Stations at which it was employed and the dates of its arrival at and departure from such Stations.

(iv)   The Military operations in which it has been engaged, and its achievements.

(v)   The names of all officers killed and wounded, and the name of any officer or soldier who has specially distinguished himself in action.

(vi)   Drafts received and despatched, their strength, dates of their arrival and departure and the names of officers who accompany them. Drafts numerically weaker than an Officer Party should not be separately specified.

(vii) Any other matter which may be considered of historical importance.

HOUNSLOW.   G. James   Major for Colonel
29.10.15   I/C Army Cyclist Corps Records Hounslow.

II

From, O.C. 14th Divisional Cyclist Company

To, Col. i/c. A.C.C. Records,
     Hounslow.

(1)   11th January 1915.

(11) This Company was recruited from all the Infantry Battalions in, and connected with, the 14th (Light) Division viz:
    6th D.C.L.I.,   7th Rifle Brigade
    6th Som.t L.I.,   8th   "   "
    10th D.L.I.,   7th K.R.R.
    6th K.O.Y.L.I.,   8th   "   "
    5th Ox & Bucks L.I., 9th   "   "
    5th K.S.L.I.,   9th Rifle Brigade
    11th King's Liverpools, 8th Devon Regt.

Owing to the fact that sufficient volunteers were not forthcoming to make up the strength of the Company from the above mentioned Battalions, C.O's were ordered to send men whether they wished to be transferred or not. Consequently many of the men received were by no means the best men in their respective battalions, and lack of discipline and dis-content were the causes of several men being re-transferred to their old Units.

However after the worst men had been weeded out and replaced by better, and after the men had become interested in the work they would be called upon to perform, and had made new friends, and a spirit of esprit de corps had

(ii continued)

become established, when I was instructed by you late in the month of April that the particulars contained in A.F. B241 would have to be complied with, no single man refused to sign the form, each man being willing to remain in the Company and anxious to proceed abroad with it.

Discipline which at first was very lax became much better as men were severely dealt with, and before the Company proceeded Overseas few cases were required to be dealt with in the Orderly Room.

(III) The Company was stationed at the following places;

"Uplands" Brook. Surrey, from 20th Jan to 24th Feb. 1915.

Badajos Barracks, Aldershot, from 24th Feb. to 18th May 1915.; proceeding Overseas on 19th May 1915.

(IV) This Company was attached to the 5th Division for instruction; the Cyclist Company of that Division instructing it in the various kinds of works performed, under the conditions of trench warfare now obtaining, by cyclists.

It first came under fire at ZILLEBEKE on 1st June 1915.

Since the Division has held part of the YPRES SALIENT the Company has been engaged on Working Parties e.g. digging Cable Trenches, constructing Machine Gun Emplacements, carrying R.E. stores; besides Salvage Work in the trenches; Road Controls,

3.

(IV continued)
and work under the A.P.M. of the Division. During the engagement on September 25/26th 2 Officers and 50 men were engaged as a Burial Party, and 2 Officers and 26 men were given sections of the road E. and W. of YPRES ~~respectively~~ to keep in a state of repair, if heavily shelled, in order that holes in, or damage caused to, the road should not impede traffic or ambulances.

The dates of Working Parties, Salvage, and other work performed, are in my War Diary, which was forwarded to you for safe custody, (~~and~~) which would give you any further information you might require under this para.

(V) Lieut. G.S.K. Baumgartner, wounded, (~~date in War Diary~~) 11th June 1915.

5148 Lance Corporal B. Shaw has been recommended by the A.P.M. 14th Division for reward on account of bravery and devotion to duty, in that, whilst serving under him he one day (date uncertain) rode several times to Divisional Headquarters under heavy shell fire to advise him of damage caused to the road by the bombardment, and although the enemy shelled continuously from 8.a.m till 5 p.m., L/Cpl. Shaw gave warning to traffic and no casualties were caused during the whole day: to do this he had to patrol the road on his cycle.

The result of the recommendation, which the Major General himself directed the A.P.M. to make to him, is not known.

4.

(vi) Draft consisting of 1 Officer (2ⁿᵈ Lieut R.F. Gwyn) and 21 other ranks arrived 14ᵗʰ Sept. 1915.

(vii) I obtained the sanction of the Major General for a distinguishing badge, colour blue, shape a square 2"x 2" to be worn in the center of the back immediately under the collar, to differentiate the cyclists from other troops in the 14ᵗʰ Division all of which wear some distinguishing badge. Cloth of this colour was purchased and the badges cut out and sewn on to the tunics on 18ᵗʰ May 1915.

F H Fowler, Capt.

COMMANDING
14TH DIVISIONAL CYCLIST COMPANY.

14TH LIGHT DIVISIONAL CYCLISTS COMPANY
Date 7.11.15
ORDERLY ROOM

14th Co

Formed 11 Jan 15

Stationed Uplands Brook
         Aldershot

Proceeded overseas 19 May 15
arrived France 20 " "
During June employed at fatigue work
& digging trenches etc.
11 June 2/Lt B ammunition wounded
July   same work
20 July 1 man wounded.
August   Salvage work & fatigues
Sep.   as above & guard over Prisoners
Oct.   do
Nov.   do

Confidential.

War Diary
of
14th Divisional Cyclist Coy.

from Dec. 1st to Dec. 31st 1915.

(Volume 8)

Army Form C. 2118.

WAR DIARY
or
INTELLIGENCE SUMMARY.
(Erase heading not required.)

Place	Date	Hour	Summary of Events and Information	Remarks and references to Appendices
WATOU	Nov 1st	8 a.m.	Loading Party 2 N.C.O's & 40 men proceeded to R.E. Park POPERINGHE returning at 4 p.m.	
"	2nd	"	ditto 2 N.C.O's & 37 men ditto	
"	3rd	8.30 a.m.	2 Lieut L.B. WILLIAMS & 30 N.C.O's & men proceeded to 14th Div Grenade School for proper of Grenade work	
"	3rd	8 a.m.	Loading Party 2 N.C.O's & 40 men proceeded to R E Park POPERINGHE returning at 4 p.m.	
"	4th	do	ditto ditto	
"	5th	do	ditto ditto	
"	"	do	Lieut N.D. Harrison & 1 man proceeded to the trenches to take up position as Intelligence Observation Officer attached to 143 Bde ditto do to 42" Bde	
"	"	do	2/Lieut L.B.Williams ditto	
"	6th	8 a.m.	Loading Party 2 N.C.O's & 35 men proceeded to R E Park POPERINGHE returning at 4 p.m.	
"	7th	"	" O men ditto	
"	8th	"	ditto ditto	
"	9th	"	ditto ditto	
"	10th	"	ditto ditto	
"	11th	"	ditto ditto	

Army Form C. 2118.

WAR DIARY
or
INTELLIGENCE SUMMARY.
(Erase heading not required.)

Instructions regarding War Diaries and Intelligence Summaries are contained in F. S. Regs., Part II. and the Staff Manual respectively. Title pages will be prepared in manuscript.

Place	Date	Hour	Summary of Events and Information	Remarks and references to Appendices
WATOU	Arch 11th	8 a.m.	Lieut S.R.K.GURNER. proceeded to Huts Construction Camp for purpose of assisting with Construction of huts camp.	
"	"	8.30 am	O.C. proceeded through YPRES for purpose of visiting CANALBANK for purpose of reporting to 6th Corps. position and types of dug-outs and present and possible accommodation in same on CANALBANK, returning to camp at about 4.00 pm.	
"	12th	8 am	Working Party 2 N.C.O & 40 men proceeded to R.E.Park POPERINGHE returning at 4 p.m.	
"	"	12.30 am	1 N.C.O & 15 men proceeded to POPERINGHE to report to R.E. 6th Corps Park.	
"	13th	8 am	Working Party 1 N.C.O & 10 men proceeded to R.E.Park POPERINGHE returning at 4 p.m.	
"	"	"	Fatigue Party 1 N.C.O & 4 men proceeded to Ordnance Stores returning at 5 p.m.	
"	"	5 pm	O.C. returned from about 4½ hrs having completed field work on CANAL BANK.	
"	14th	8 am	Working Party 2. N.C.O & 40 men proceeded to R.E.Park POPERINGHE returning at 4 p.m.	
"	"	"	Fatigue Party 1 N.C.O & 6 men proceeded to Ordnance Stores returning at 5 p.m.	
"	"	"	O.C. made out full report as to present & possible accommodation on YSER CANAL BANK, YPRES, in dug-outs, & types of same forwarded to about H.Qtrs. with plan at scale of 1/1800 showing their position and types, for 6th Corps.	
"	15th	8 a.m.	Working Party 2 N.C.O & 40 men proceeded to R.E.Park POPERINGHE returning at 4 p.m.	

WAR DIARY
or
INTELLIGENCE SUMMARY.

(Erase heading not required.)

Army Form C. 2118.

Place	Date	Hour	Summary of Events and Information	Remarks and references to Appendices
WA10J	Feb 15th	8a.m.	Fatigue Party 1 N.C.O & 10 men proceeded to Ordnance Stores returning at 5 p.m. Orders were received from the Division to return all plans & maps of the trenches & neighbourhood, also to get the Unit complete to War Estab.' for a move. O.C. being required to furnish a daily report as to the progress of same.	III
"	"	2 p.m.	LIEUT. H.D. HARRISON & 1 man returned from trenches on Division being relieved	III
"	16th	8 a.m.	2 Lieut L.B. WILLIAMS + 1 man ditto	III
"	"	"	Loading Party 2 N.C.O & 40 men proceeded to R.E. Pads POPERINGHE returning at 4 p.m.	III
"	17th	"	Fatigue Party 1 N.C.O & 10 men proceeded to Ordnance Stores returning at 5 p.m. ditto	III
"	"	"	ditto	III
"	"	8 a.m.	Loading Party 2 N.C.O & 40 men proceeded to R.E. Pads POPERINGHE returning at 4 p.m.	III
"	"	2 p.m.	Lieut H.A. ROBERTSON & 4 men returned from 14th Bn Essex School	III
"	18th	8 a.m.	Fatigue Party 1 N.C.O & 10 men proceeded to Ordnance Stores returning at 5 p.m.	III
"	"	"	Lieut A.L. NARE & 1 Platoon proceeded to 14th Divs H.Qrs for duty (guards & fatigue)	III
"	"	"	Defence scheme orders were received in case enemy made hostile attack on 6th Corps front, 14th Division being in Corps Reserve.	III

WAR DIARY or INTELLIGENCE SUMMARY

Army Form C. 2118.

Place	Date	Hour	Summary of Events and Information	Remarks and references to Appendices
WR 10 J	Feb 19	7 a.m.	Information received that Engineers attendants gas on 6th Corps front & that was fatal.	H.S.T.
"	"	7.30	Orders received from Division to be prepared to put into force the system of control posts mentioned in Defence Scheme received 18th inst.	H.S.T.
"	"	8 a.m.	Fatigue party 1 N.C.O. & 10 men provided to Ordnance	H.S.T.
"	"	4.30 p.m.	Orders received from Division that no further need for this unit to stand to.	H.S.T.
"	20th	8 a.m.	Fatigue party 1 N.C.O. & 10 men proceeded to Ordnance Stores returning at 5 p.m.	H.S.T.
"	21st	"	ditto	H.S.T.
"	"	"	O.C. & Lieut. S.R.K. GURNER present on leave.	H.S.T.
"	"	"	2/Lieut L.B. WILLIAMS proceeded to Hutcavintin Camp to prepare for erecting with construction Huts.	H.S.T.
"	22nd	8 a.m.	Fatigue party 1 N.C.O. & 10 men proceeded to Ordnance Stores returning at 5 p.m. Lieut S. SHEPHERD & 14 men returned to Unit from doing duty on Road Control.	H.S.T.
"	23rd	8 a.m.	Fatigue party 1 N.C.O. & 10 men proceeded to Ordnance Stores returning at 5 p.m.	H.S.T.
"	24th	do	ditto	ditto
"	25th	do	ditto	ditto

WAR DIARY or INTELLIGENCE SUMMARY

Army Form C. 2118.

Place	Date	Hour	Summary of Events and Information	Remarks and references to Appendices
WATOU	25th	4.30	All orders regarding the move of the Unit were cancelled.	1st 15/16
"	26th	8 a.m.	Fatigue Party 1 N.C.O. + 10 men proceeded to Ordnance Stores returning at 2 p.m.	2 15/16
"	27th	"	ditto	"
"	"	"	Lieut H.D. HARRISON proceeded to Divn H.Q. 263 returning about 3.30 p.m.	
"	"	12 noon	Lieut H.A. Robertson + 4 men proceeded to 1st Divn Grenade School for duty	
"	28th	9 a.m.	Lieut S. SHEPHERD reconnoitred Groups Nos 1–4 in Defences Béthune	
"	29th	6 p.m.	10 men proceeded to VLAMERTINGHE O.C. & Lieut S.R.K. GURNER arrived at BOULOGNE at 2.30 p.m.	
"	30th	8 a.m.	Billeting party proceeded to STE SIXTE to take over billets for this Unit	
"	"	7.15 a.m.	O.C. + Lieut S.R.K. GURNER left BOULOGNE	
"	"	10 a.m.	Warders & Garrisons posted to Groups 1–4 of fortified posts	
"	"	"	ditto also to fortified post 6–10 in neighbourhood of ELVERTINGHE	
"	31st	3 a.m.	O.C. & Lieut S.R.K. GURNER returned from leave	
"	"	11 a.m.	Company moved into new billets at CONVENT STE SIXTE	

14th strike: Gehsts
bl 9
Tan 716

Confidential

War Diary
of
14th Divisional Cyclist Coy.

from January 1st to January 31st 1916.

(Volume 9)

Army Form C. 2118.

WAR DIARY
or
INTELLIGENCE SUMMARY.
(Erase heading not required.)

Place	Date	Hour	Summary of Events and Information	Remarks and references to Appendices
STE SIXTE	Jan/1916. 1		General fatigue in new billet	AJ
"	2		do	AJ
"	3	9 a.m.	O.C. made a reconnaissance of Fortified & Garrison Posts between STE SIXTE and ELVERDINGHE.	AJ
"	4	10 a.m.	O.C. inspected Group 1 & 2 Fortified Posts to see what repairs were needed	AJ
"	"		Lieut H.A. ROBERTSON inspected Group 3 & 4. do	AJ
"	"		Lieut S.R.K. GURNER inspected POSTS 7. 8. 9 & 10. do	AJ
"	5th	9 a.m.	Working Party 1 N.C.O & 10 men proceeded to Group 2 of Fortified Posts.	AJ
"	6th	do.	do 1 N.C.O & 24 men do	AJ
"	7. "	do.	do do	AJ
"	8 "	do	do do	AJ
"	"	do.	O.C. proceeded with General Staff Officer (3) through BRIELEN. 14th Division for purpose of reconnoitring a position for an Observation Post for 42nd Brigade.	AJ
"	"	do	Cpl REED proceeded to 41st Brigade to relieve Intelligence observer of Duke of Lancaster Yeomanry. (14th Divisional Cavalry) BRIELEN. & CANAL BANK	AJ

WAR DIARY
or
INTELLIGENCE SUMMARY.
(Erase heading not required.)

Army Form C. 2118.

Place	Date	Hour	Summary of Events and Information	Remarks and references to Appendices
STE SIXTE	Jan 8	10 a.m.	Smoke Helmet inspection and report made to Division	
"	9	3 p.m.	Church Parade	
"	10	11 a.m.	O.C. & 1 man proceeded to CANAL BANK to take up position as Intelligence Observation Officers attached to 42nd Bde.	
"	"	"	1 man proceeded to 41st Bde. to relieve Intelligence observer of 14th Divt Cavalry	
"	"	12 noon	Company Parade	
"	"	9 p.m.	Working Party 1 N.C.O. & 24 men proceeded to Group 2 of Fortified Posts.	
"	11th	do	do	
"	"	11 a.m.	Lieut S.R.K. GURNER proceeded to 43rd Bde. to take up position as Intelligence Observation Officer.	
"	"	3 p.m.	15 men returned from Divl. Headquarters	
"	12	11 a.m.	do	
"	"	9 "	do	
"	13th	9 a.m.	Working party 1 N.C.O. & 2 4 men proceeded to Group 2 of Fortified Posts.	
"	"	"	do	
"	"	"	do	

WAR DIARY or INTELLIGENCE SUMMARY

Army Form C. 2118.

Place	Date	Hour	Summary of Events and Information	Remarks and references to Appendices
STE SIXTE	Jan 14	9 a.m.	Working party 1 N.C.O & 24 men proceeded to Group 2 of Fortified Posts	A.S.C.
"	15th	"	do	
"	16th	10.15	Church Parade	A.S.C.
"	17th	9 a.m.	Working party 1 N.C.O & 24 men proceeded to Group 2 of Fortified Posts	
"	18th	"	do	
"	19	"	do	A.S.C.
"	"	"	1 N.C.O & 3 men proceeded to BRIELEN for purpose of salvage work	
"	20	"	1 N.C.O & 5 men do	A.S.C.
"	"	"	Working party 1 N.C.O. & 24 men proceeded to Group 2 of Fortified Posts	
"	21	"	do	
"	"	"	1 N.C.O & 5 men proceeded to BRIELEN for purpose of salvage work	A.S.C.
"	22nd	"	Working party 1 N.C.O & 24 men proceeded to Group 2 of Fortified Posts	A.S.C.
"	23rd	10 a.m.	Church Parade	A.S.C.
"	24th	9 a.m.	Working party 1 N.C.O. & 24 men proceeded to Group 2 of Fortified Posts	A.S.C.
"	25	"	do	
"	"	10 a.m.	1 N.C.O & 6 men proceeded to Report to G.O.C. 42nd Bde for purpose of Salvage Work.	A.S.C.

WAR DIARY
or
INTELLIGENCE SUMMARY.

Army Form C. 2118.

Place	Date	Hour	Summary of Events and Information	Remarks and references to Appendices
St Siat	Jan 26	9 a.m.	1 N.C.O. & 24 men as Working Party proceeded to Group 2 of Fortified Posts	W.J.R.
"	27	"	1 N.C.O & 7 men proceeded to BRIELEN for purpose of salvage work returning at 5 p.m.	W.J.R.
"	28	-	Working Party 1 N.C.O & 24 men proceeded to Group 2 of Fortified Posts	W.J.R.
"	29	12 noon	Company inspection	W.J.R.
"	30	9.30 a.m	Church Parade	
"	"	9 a.m.	Lieut H.A. ROBERTSON proceeded to 42nd Bde to relieve O.C. as Intelligence observation officer. O.C. returned at 6 p.m.	W.J.
"	"	"	2/Lieut R.F. GWYN. proceeded to 43rd Bde to relieve Lieut. S.R.K. GURNER as Intelligence observation officer. Lieut S.R.K GURNER returned at 6 p.m.	W.J.
"	31	8.30	2/Lieut L.B. WILLIAMS & 20 N.C.O & men proceeded to BRIELEN for purpose of salvage work.	W.J.
"	"	3 p.m	1 N.C.O & 14 men proceeded to report to A.P.M. 14th Division for duty	W.J

Confidential.

War Diary
of 14th Divisional Cyclist Coy.

from Feby 1st 1916 to Feby 29th 1916.

(Volume 10)

Army Form C. 2118.

WAR DIARY
or
INTELLIGENCE SUMMARY.
(Erase heading not required.)

Instructions regarding War Diaries and Intelligence Summaries are contained in F.S. Regs., Part II. and the Staff Manual respectively. Title pages will be prepared in manuscript.

Place	Date 1916	Hour	Summary of Events and Information	Remarks and references to Appendices
STE SIXTE	Feby 1	9 am	1 N.C.O. + 24 men proceeded to the neighbourhood of ELVERDINGHE for purpose of salvage work.	XII
"	2	10 am	Lecture delivered by O.C. + 2nd in Command to 30 N.C.O.'s + men detailed as Guides on duty they would have to perform in the event of a battle attack on 14th Divl. sector	XII
"	3	5 p	1 N.C.O. & 14 men returned from A.C.M. 14th Division	XII
"	"	9 am	1 N.C.O. & 30 men proceeded to the neighbourhood of ELVERDINGHE for purpose of salvage	XII
"	4	9 am	Fatigue Party 1 N.C.O. 12 men proceeded to 49th Vet. Section F.12.a.4.0 (sheet 28 Belgium) for purpose of clearing Camp & returning Stores to Ordnance at POPERINGHE	XII
"	5	9 am	1 N.C.O. & 30 men proceeded to neighbourhood of ELVERDINGHE for purpose ditto	XII
"	6	9 am	Squad by ditto	XII
"	"	10 am	Church Parade	XII
"	7	9.30 am	Smoke Helmet Inspection.	XII
"	"	"	1 N.C.O. & 4 men proceeded to 49th Vet Section F.12.a.4.0 for purpose of loading R.E. Stores on waggons to bring to three billets for safe custody,	XII
"	8	3.30 pm	Operation could not be sp. visited for removal of this division from this area.	XII
"	"	9.30 am	Company Inspection	XII
"	"	11.30 am	Kit inspection by O.C.	XII

1577 Wt. W10791/1773 500,000 1/15 D. D. & L. A.D.S.S./Forms/C. 2118.

WAR DIARY
or
INTELLIGENCE SUMMARY.
(Erase heading not required.)

Army Form C. 2118.

Place	Date 1916 Feb	Hour	Summary of Events and Information	Remarks and references to Appendices
STE. SIXTE	9	12 noon	Company Inspection.	N.I.
"	"	2p.m.	Wardens & Garrisons posted to Groups 1-4 of Fortified Posts relieved by 20th Divn.	N.I.
"	10	12 noon	Company Inspection.	N.I.
"	"	2p.m.	Garrisons of Posts P.7-10. relieved by 20th Division.	N.I.
"	"	6p.m.	Lieut. H.A. ROBERTSON. attached to 42nd. Bde as 2nd. Observation Officer. & 1 man, returned from Observing on CANAL BANK. on Division being relieved by 20th Divn.	N.I.
"	11 "	2p.m.	M.C.O & 6 men returned from 42nd Bde. H.Q. 2lt. having finished salvage work.	N.I.
"	"	6p.m.	2/Lieut. R.H. GWYN. attached to 43rd. Bde as 2nd. Observation Officer returned from Observing on CANAL BANK on Division being relieved by 20th Divn.	N.I.
"	"	3p.m.	2/Lieut. L.B. WILLIAMS & 9 men proceeded to BRIELEN in accordance with Divnl. Orders for purpose of relieving Guns Boots from Units of this Division and handing over to 20th Division.	N.I.
"	"	"	Lieut S.R.K. GURNER & 5 men proceeded to POPERINGHE in accordance with Divnl Orders for purpose of receiving Guns Boots from Units of this Division and handing over to 20th Division.	N.I.
"	"	8p.m.	1 N.C.O & 10 men returned to duty from A.P.M. 14th Division on being relieved by 20th Division.	N.I.

WAR DIARY
or
INTELLIGENCE SUMMARY.

Army Form C. 2118.

Place	Date 1916	Hour	Summary of Events and Information	Remarks and references to Appendices
STE SIXTE	12th	9.40am	Company moved into new billets at ESQUELBECQ arriving at 5 p.m.	C.8.a.9.6 Sheet 27 (BELGIUM)
ESQUELBECQ	13th	5 p.m.	1 N.C.O. & 12 men returned to duty from A.P.M. 14th Division.	W.J.
"	14th	10 am	1 N.C.O. & 5 men reported to A.P.M. for duty.	W.J.
"	"	12 noon	Company Inspection	W.J.
"	15th	"	do.	W.J.
"	16th	"	do.	W.J.
"	17th	"	do.	W.J.
"	"	3 p.m.	Company Pay	W.J.
"	18th	12 am	G.O.C. visited the Coy. H.Q. 2bis and complemented the 10 divisional Intelligence Observers (Officers & men) on the good work done during the period the 10 Division were in the trenches N of YPRES	W.J.
"	19th	6 p.m.	Coy marched from ESQUELBECQ	W.J.
"	"	8 p.m.	do arrived at CASSEL	W.J.
"	"	10.15 p.m.	do left CASSEL by train	W.J.
"	20th	9 a.m.	Train arrived at LONGUEAU STATION, AMIENS.	W.J.

Army Form C. 2118.

WAR DIARY
or
INTELLIGENCE SUMMARY.
(Erase heading not required.)

Instructions regarding War Diaries and Intelligence Summaries are contained in F. S. Regs., Part II. and the Staff Manual respectively. Title pages will be prepared in manuscript.

Place	Date	Hour	Summary of Events and Information	Remarks and references to Appendices
AMIENS.	20th Feb	1 p.m.	Coy arrived at new billets at VILLERS BOCAGE (Reference Map AMIENS sheet 17)	NJ.
VILLERS BOCAGE	21st	12 noon	Company Inspection. Div. G.O.C. Inspected the Unit and billets.	NJ.
VILLERS BOCAGE	22nd	9.30 a.m.	do	NJ.
"	"	10 a.m.	Route march.	NJ.
"	23rd	9.30 a.m.	Smoke Helmet inspection. Snow commenced to fall at mid-day	NJ.
"	24th	12.30 p.m.	Brigade O.C. called out to 11th Battn Kings Liverpool Reg. to receive orders for Bn. move in the morning	NJ.
"	24th	9.30	Coy marched from VILLERS BOCAGE via TALMAS and BEAUVAL to GÉZAINCOURT.	NJ.
"	"	11.45 a.m.	do arrived at GÉZAINCOURT. (Reference Map No. 11 LENS) and took up billets	NJ.
GEZAINCOURT	25th	9.30 a.m.	Coy marched from do via DOULLENS - BOUQUEMAISON - IVERGNY to SUS ST LEGER. March was performed in a blizzard, snow commencing to fall at 10 a.m. & continued all day	NJ.
SUS ST LEGER	25th	1.30 p.m.	Unit arrived at SUS ST LEGER and took up billets, waggon containing supplies did not arrive owing to Div. Train being held up by state of roads.	NJ.
"	26th	12 noon	Company inspection	NJ.
"	27th	9 a.m.	Company employed in clearing snow away in main road through the village	NJ.
"	28	9.30 a.m.	Company marched from SUS ST LEGER via SOMORIN to BARLY (Reference map LENS No 11); arrived at 10.30 a.m. and took up billets; snow commenced to thaw.	NJ.

1577 Wt.W10791/1773 500,000 1/15 D.D.&L.   A.D.S.S./Forms/C. 2118.

Army Form C. 2118.

WAR DIARY
or
INTELLIGENCE SUMMARY.
(Erase heading not required.)

Instructions regarding War Diaries and Intelligence Summaries are contained in F. S. Regs., Part II. and the Staff Manual respectively. Title pages will be prepared in manuscript.

Place	Date	Hour	Summary of Events and Information	Remarks and references to Appendices
BARLY.	July 29	9 a.m.	O.C took over duties as Town Major. BARLY.	
		12 noon	Company Inspection.	

14 Div Cyclist
Vol II

Confidential

War Diary
of
14th Divisional Cyclist Coy.

from March 1st to March 31st 1916

(Volume II)

Army Form C. 2118.

WAR DIARY
or
INTELLIGENCE SUMMARY.
(Erase heading not required.)

Instructions regarding War Diaries and Intelligence Summaries are contained in F.S. Regs., Part II. and the Staff Manual respectively. Title pages will be prepared in manuscript.

Place	Date	Hour	Summary of Events and Information	Remarks and references to Appendices
BARLY	Mch 1	9am	Lieut H.D. HARRISON & Lieut S.R.K. GURNER proceeded to Fumy Line for purpose of making a reconnaissance or observation intelligence posts on front taken over by 14th Division in vicinity of ARRAS	S.I.
"	"	1.30pm	2/Lt R.T. George & 30 men proceeded to DAINVILLE for purpose of controlling traffic, under orders of A.P.M. 14th Division	S.I.
"	1st	2.30pm	Rifles issued for hostile Vet Section 14th Division these were taken over on 2nd inst.	S.I.
"	"	"	do do No 3 Coy Train	S.I.
"	2nd	10am	Company Inspection	S.I.
"	"	10.30am	do drill	S.I.
"	3rd	10am	Rifles issued for No 1 Coy Train	S.I.
"	"	"	Company Inspection	S.I.
"	"	"	do drill	S.I.
"	"	"	2 N.C.O's & 10 men proceeded to FOSSEUX to report to A.P.M. 6th Corps for duty	S.I.
"	4th	5pm	1 Official & 52 men from 1st Corps were attached to this Unit for rations	S.I.
"	"	11am	Company Pay	S.I.
"	4th	9am	Lieut H.D. HARRISON & L/Cpl L.D. WILLIAMS & 2 men reported to Div No 2 at BERNEVILLE for examination but owing to fall of snow they returned to BARLY as observing was not possible.	S.I.

WAR DIARY or INTELLIGENCE SUMMARY.

Army Form C. 2118.

Place	Date	Hour	Summary of Events and Information	Remarks and references to Appendices
BARLY	Mar 5th	11 a.m.	Church Parade	
"	" 6th	12 m	Billets found for 14th D.A.C.	
"		9 a.m.	Lieut H.D. HARRISON & 1 N.C.O proceeded to RUE JEANNE D'ARC ARRAS to take up position as Divit Intelligence Observers attached to 41st Infantry Bde. 2nd Lieut L.B. WILLIAMS & 1 N.C.O proceeded to DAINVILLE to take up position as Divit Intelligence Observers attached to 11th LIVERPOOLS Regt.	
"	" 7th	10 a.m.	Company Inspection. 14th D.A.C took up billets allotted to them	
"	"		ditto	
"	"	2 p.m.	Smoke Helmet inspection	
"	" 8th	10 a.m.	Company Inspection	
"		2 p.m. to 10 a.m.	Route march A.Co's & B men proceeded to 14th Divit Ration dumps in the vicinity of WANQUETIN, for purpose of gaining information attending at 9 a.m. Company Inspection ditto drill	
"	" 9th	2 p.m.		
"	" 9th	8 p.m.	2 N.C.O's & 6 men proceeded to 14th Divit Ration dumps in the vicinity of WANQUETIN for purpose of gaining Rations attaining at 9 a.m.	
"	" 10th	10 a.m.	Company Inspection	

WAR DIARY or INTELLIGENCE SUMMARY.

Army Form C. 2118.

Place	Date	Hour	Summary of Events and Information	Remarks and references to Appendices
BARLY	Aug 10th	2 p.m.	Company drill	XJ
"	11th	10 a.m.	Company Inspection	XJ
"	"	2 p.m.	Company drill	XJ
"	12th	10 a.m.	Report sent to Division that 5 Enemy's aeroplanes visited BARLY and dropped a bomb but no damage was done; they remained from 8 a.m. to 8.20 a.m. the report was sent in by O.C. as Administrative Commandant.	XJ XJ
"	"	2.30 p.m.	Church Parade	XJ
"	13th	10 a.m.	Company Inspection	XJ
"	"	2 p.m.	do	XJ
"	"	4 p.m.	1 N.C.O. & 10 men proceeded to DAINVILLE to report to 2/Lt L.B. WILLIAMS for purpose of constructing an O.P. the spot selected for observing for Intelligence purposes had no cover and the Observation Officer had to construct an O.P. for himself. A full report was furnished to General Staff 14th Div. on suspicious lights observed between 9.50 p.m. and 12 midnight 12th inst. in the Church Tower, BARLY by O.C. in his capacity of Administrative Commandant	XJ XJ
"	14th	8 a.m.	1 N.C.O. & 3 men proceeded to ARRAS to report to LIEUT. HARRISON Divisional Intelligence Observation Officer to assist in strengthening observing the Observation Post. They returned at 5 p.m.	XJ XJ

WAR DIARY
or
INTELLIGENCE SUMMARY.
(Erase heading not required.)

Army Form C. 2118.

Place	Date	Hour	Summary of Events and Information	Remarks and references to Appendices
BARLY	Inst. 14th	2.30	A message having been received from Div¹ Head Quarters that N.C.O.s and men from this Unit would be required to guide strange troops up to the trenches in the event of an action, in order to re-inforce our Division, LIEUT. H.A. ROBERTSON took a party of N.C.O.s as far as DAINVILLE in order to reconnoitre the 2nd and 3rd line of defence behind the Div. sector; they returned at 7 p.m.	XVI.
	14th	4 p.m.	N.C.O. + 10 men proceeded to DAINVILLE to continue constructing an O.P. for 2nd LIEUT. L.B. WILLIAMS of this Unit.	XVI.
	15th	10.30	LIEUT ROBERTSON took his party of N.C.O.s to ARRAS in order to ascertain the exact positions of the communication trenches leading to our front line.	XVI.
	"	4 p.m.	1 N.C.O. 10 men proceeded to DAINVILLE to continue constructing an O.P. for 2nd LIEUT L.B. WILLIAMS of this Unit.	XVI.
	16th	4 p.m.	1 N.C.O. + 15 men proceeded to DAINVILLE to continue completing an O.P. for 2nd LIEUT L.B. WILLIAMS of this Unit.	XVI.
	"	6.30 p.m.	4 Bombers returned to this Unit for duty from 2 P.M. 114th Division as the result of a letter from O.C. requesting that the men trained as grenadiers in this Unit and are fit for duty might be returned, as they formed part of the Divisional Reserve of Bombers. 4 men being sent to him to replace them.	XVI.

Army Form C. 2118.

WAR DIARY
or
INTELLIGENCE SUMMARY.
(Erase heading not required.)

Instructions regarding War Diaries and Intelligence Summaries are contained in F.S. Regs., Part II. and the Staff Manual respectively. Title pages will be prepared in manuscript.

Place	Date	Hour	Summary of Events and Information	Remarks and references to Appendices
BARLY.	Feb. 17th	11 a.m.	7 Bombers returned to Unit for duty from A.P.M. 6th Corps as the result of a letter from O.C. regretting that there were many as grenadiers in this Unit and sent to him for duty, might be returned, as they formed part of the Divisional Reserve of Bombers. 7 men being sent to him to replace them.	XV
"	"	4 p.m.	1 N.C.O. & 17 men proceeded to DAINVILLE to continue constructing an O.P. for 2/Lieut L.B. WILLIAMS of this Unit.	XV XVI XVII
"	18th	12 noon	Company inspection.	XV
"	"	2.30 p.m.	Lecture given on bombing by the Divisional Grenade Officer.	XV
"	18th		hied S.R.R. GURNER a billeting party proceeded to FOSSEUX to report to Armentières Command with reference to billets; orders being received from Division for this Unit to move to that village.	XV
"	19th	10 a.m.	Company marched from BARLY to FOSSEUX arriving at 10.30 a.m. & took up billets.	XV
"	"	11 a.m.	O.C. handed over the duties of Town Major BARLY to Major KNIGHT 1/3rd West LANCS. FIELD AMBULANCE; remaining in BARLY till 12.40 p.m. in order to report to 14th Division that all Units were clear of BARLY.	XVI

1577 Wt.W10791/1773 500,000 1/15 D.D.&L. A.D.S.S./Forms/C. 2118.

Army Form C. 2118.

WAR DIARY
or
INTELLIGENCE SUMMARY.
(Erase heading not required.)

Place	Date	Hour	Summary of Events and Information	Remarks and references to Appendices
FOSSEUX	March 19	4pm	1 N.C.O & 17 men proceeded to DAINVILLE to continue constructing an O.P. for 2/Lieut L.B. WILLIAMS of this Unit.	IV
"	"	5pm	1 N.C.O & 20 men proceeded to DAINVILLE to report to LIEUT H.D. HARRISON for purpose of carrying sandbags to his O.P. in order to strengthen it	IV
"	20th	1 p.m.	3 N.C.O & 9 men proceeded to 14th Division refilling point J23.6. on AVESNES - HARBARCQ ROAD. Sheet 51c. for purpose of guarding supplies returning at 9.a.m 21st inst.	IV
"	21st	5 a.m	2 N.C.O & 40 men proceeded to SAULTY to report to Railway Supply Officer for purpose of loading supplies returning at 12.30 p.m.	IV
"	"	2.30 pm	Company pay	IV
"	"	3 pm	Smoke Helmet inspection	IV
"	22nd	5 a.m	1 N.C.O & 25 men proceeded to SAULTY to report to Railway Supply Officer for purpose of loading supplies returning at 4.30 p.m.	IV
"	"	2 pm	O.C. received message asking him to meet Divisional N.C.O. when he was informed that he would be attached to them for instruction in Staff duties.	IV
"	23rd	5 a.m	1 N.C.O & 25 men proceeded to SAULTY to report to Railway Supply Officer for purpose of loading supplies returning at 4.30 p.m.	SMG

WAR DIARY
or
INTELLIGENCE SUMMARY
(Erase heading not required.)

Army Form C. 2118

Place	Date	Hour	Summary of Events and Information	Remarks and references to Appendices
FOSSEUX	March 23	5pm	N.C.O & 15 men proceeded to DAINVILLE to report to Lieut H.D. HARRISON for purpose of loading waggons with material for repairing his O.P.	SRK?
"	23rd		Heavy fall of snow fell during night.	
"	24		O.C. commenced a reconnaissance of the accommodation & Staff grids in the Divisional Area between BERNEVILLE and DAINVILLE.	SRK?
"		do	1 N.C.O & 15 men proceeded to DAINVILLE to report to Lieut H.D. Harrison for purpose of loading waggons with material for repairing his O.P.	
"	25	10 am	1 N.C.O & 1 man proceeded to HAUTEVILLE to report to O.C. 14" Dw. Grenade School for duty	SPK?
"	26	11.15am	Church Parade.	
"	27	10 am	Company inspection	SPK?
"	28	do	do	SPK?
"	29	9.30am	33 N.C.O's & men proceeded through ARRAS for purpose of reconnoitring communication trenches, since the 15th inst this party has availed itself of every suitable day for this work and its training is now complete.	SPK?
"	30	10 az	Company inspection	W.
"	"		O.C. finished reconnaissance of accommodation in dug-outs and handed report with. theretofore upon same to the Staff.	W.
"	31	12 am	Company inspection W.C. returned from BERNEVILLE.	W.

14 Divs Cyclists
Vol 12

Confidential.

War Diary

of

14th Divisional Cyclist Coy.

from April 1st to April 30th 1916.

(Volume 12)

Army Form C. 2118

WAR DIARY
or
INTELLIGENCE SUMMARY
(Erase heading not required.)

Instructions regarding War Diaries and Intelligence Summaries are contained in F. S. Regs., Part II. and the Staff Manual respectively. Title Pages will be prepared in manuscript.

Place	Date April	Hour	Summary of Events and Information	Remarks and references to Appendices
FOSSEUX	1st	10 am	Company inspection. OC and Lieut GURNER into ARRAS for the purpose of visiting the observation post occupied at present by Lieut HARRISON of this Unit.	XI
"	"	6pm	N.C.Os & men proceeded through ARRAS for purpose of reconnoitring communication trenches by night.	XI
"	2nd	11 am	Church parade.	XI
"	3rd	10 am	Company inspection	XI
"	4th	10 am	Company inspection	XI
"	"	2.30pm	Company pay.	XI
"	"	6pm	N.C.Os & men proceeded through ARRAS to purpose of reconnoitring communication trenches by night.	XI
"	5th	10 am	Company inspection.	XI
"	6th	8.30 am	50 N.C.Os & men proceeded to HAUTEVILLE for baths.	XI
"	"	10 am	Company inspection	XI
"	7th	9.30 am	50 N.C.Os & men proceeded to HAUTEVILLE for baths.	XI
"	"	2pm	Pte BAMFORD was forwarded to 1st Divisional Base depot on completion of 3 months field punishment No 1 to serve on a reinforcement to this Unit.	XI

WAR DIARY
or
INTELLIGENCE SUMMARY

(Erase heading not required.)

Army Form C. 2118

Place	Date	Hour	Summary of Events and Information	Remarks and references to Appendices
FOSSEUX	7th	5.30 pm	O.C. proceeded to England on leave.	
	8th	10 am	Company commenced short course of musketry: Owing to the fact that the men of this Unit have not been called upon to fire or use their rifles the O.C. requested authority from Divn Headquarters to expend 50 rounds of S.A.A. per man in order to put them through a course of musketry, to prevent them getting out of practice.	
	9th	11 am	Church parade.	
	10th	10 am	Company inspection.	
		10.15 am	Company had firing practice.	
	11th	10 am	Company inspection	
	12th	10 am	Company inspection: 2nd Lieut FINNEY reported as reinforcement.	
	13th	10 am	Company inspection	
		10.15	Firing practice morning and afternoon.	
		5.30 am	40 men proceeded to HAUTEVILLE for baths.	
	14th	6.30 am	50 men proceeded to HAUTEVILLE for baths.	
		9.30 am	1 NCO + 12 men met Lieut FINNEY at AVESNES for purpose of practising tactical work.	
		2.30 pm	1 NCO + 12 men met Lt FINNEY at AVESNES for purpose of practising tactical work.	

Army Form C. 2118

WAR DIARY
or
INTELLIGENCE SUMMARY
(Erase heading not required.)

Instructions regarding War Diaries and Intelligence Summaries are contained in F.S. Regs., Part II. and the Staff Manual respectively. Title Pages will be prepared in manuscript.

Place	Date	Hour	Summary of Events and Information	Remarks and references to Appendices
FOSSEUX	Apl 15th	9.30 am	Firing practice	XI
		2.30 pm	Firing practice	XI
"	16th	10.30 am	Church parade for Weslyanuals	XI
			Lieut WILLIAMS returned from work of observation from which he was withdrawn for training under Col CHEYNE	XI
			Lieut GWYNN returned from duties in assisting APM 14th Division	XI
			from which he was withdrawn in order to take up training under Col CHEYNE	XI
			Lieut HARRISON returned from observation for training under Col CHEYNE.	XI
"	17th	9.30 am	Officers proceeded to NOYELLE VION and there met Col CHEYNE for the purpose of commencing a course under that officer, he having been detailed by Third Army to train Divisional Mounted Troops of VI Corps in Tactics.	XI
		2.30 pm	N.C.O instructed their platoons in Arm drill & physical training	XI
"	18th	2.30 pm	O.C. returned from leave.	XI
		2.30 pm	Company inspection in huts owing to rainy weather.	XI
"	19th	9 am	4 Officers proceeded to FILES CAMP FARM for further training in Tactics for open warfare.	XI
		10 am	Platoon sergeants inspected their platoons.	XII

Army Form C. 2118

WAR DIARY
or
INTELLIGENCE SUMMARY
(Erase heading not required.)

Place	Date	Hour	Summary of Events and Information	Remarks and references to Appendices
FOSSEUX	April 19th	11 pm	Message received from Div: stating that only those Officers who could ride horses would attend course under Col Cheyne	W.J.
"	20th	9 am	O.C. proceeded to FILES CAMP FARM on horseback to take part in course under Col Cheyne.	W.J.
"	"	9 am 10.30 am	60 men proceeded to HAUTEVILLE for bath	W.J.
"	"	4 pm	Pte BAMFORD was returned to this Unit from base as reinforcement	W.J.
"	"	5 pm	Company fray.	W.J.
"	21st	9 am	O.C. proceeded to AVESNES to take part in course under Col CHEYNE	W.J.
"	"	9.30 am to 11 am	60 men proceeded to HAUTEVILLE for bath	W.J.
"	"	2 pm	Company inspection	W.J.
"	"	2.30 pm	Officers took their respective platoons to adjacent parts of Country for map reading and usual training returning at 4.30 p.m.	W.J.
"	22nd	9.30 am	O.C. proceeded to AVESNES for Staff Ride under Col CHEYNE	W.J.
"	"	10.30 am	Company inspection	W.J.
"	"	2.30	Sergt SHAW proceeded to Div Observation Post, attached to HM King's Royal Rifles for relief	W.J.
"	23rd	11 am	Church parade	W.J.

Army Form C. 2118

WAR DIARY
or
INTELLIGENCE SUMMARY
(Erase heading not required.)

Place	Date Apl	Hour	Summary of Events and Information	Remarks and references to Appendices
FOSSEUX	24th	11.0 am	OC and four officers met Lt/Col CHEYNE at FOSSEUX to take part in course	XI
		10 am	Company inspection	XI
	25th	2/m	LIEUT. H.A. ROBERTSON reported at Div! Grenade School as an Instructor (temporary)	XI
		10 am	Officers & men proceeded to GRANDE ROULCOURT for tactical scheme under Lt/Col CHEYNE	XI
	26th	10 am	Officers & men proceeded to GRANDE ROULCOURT for tactical scheme under Lt/Col CHEYNE	XII
	"	1.30 pm	2nd Lieut. E. JOBLING reported for duty.	
	27th	10 am	Officers and men proceeded to SOMBRIN for tactical scheme under Lt/Col CHEYNE.	XIII
	28th		Corp MOLLOY proceeded to Divisional Observation Post, attached to 61st Field Coy R.E. for instruction	XIV
		10 pm	Officers and NCOs proceeded to IZEL LES HAMEAU for tactical scheme under Lt/Col CHEYNE.	XV
	29th	10 am	Company inspection	XVI
		10.30	Lecture by C.O. to Company on lessons gained during the Course under Lt/Col CHEYNE	XVII

Confidential

War Diary
of
14th Divisional Cyclist Coy.

from May 1st to May 11th 1916.

(Volume 13)

WAR DIARY
or
INTELLIGENCE SUMMARY

Army Form C. 2118.

Place	Date	Hour	Summary of Events and Information	Remarks and references to Appendices
FOSSEUX	May 1st	10 a.m.	Officers & men proceeded to MANIN for tactical scheme under Lt Col CHEYNE	
"		6 p.m.	Company Pay.	
"	2nd	10.30 a.m.	Officers & N.C.Os attended lecture given by Lt Col CHEYNE at FOSSEUX.	
"		6 p.m.	Night operations in vicinity of FOSSEUX	
"	3rd	11.30 a.m.	Officers & N.C.Os attended lecture given by Lt Col CHEYNE at FOSSEUX.	
"		1.30 p.m.	Officers & N.C.Os proceeded to HAUTEVILLE for tactical scheme under Lt Col CHEYNE	
"	4th	9 a.m.	Officers & N.C.Os proceeded to HERMAVILLE for tactical scheme under Lt Col CHEYNE	
"		12 noon	Lieut S.R.K. GURNER & billeting party proceeded to IZEL-LEZ-HAMEAU to obtain billets for Company	
"	5th	10.30 a.m.	Company marched from FOSSEUX to IZEL-LEZ-HAMEAU arriving at 12.30 pm & took up new billets	
"		9 a.m.	Lieut H.D. HARRISON proceeded to take part in tactical scheme under Lt Col CHEYNE in vicinity of POMMERA.	
IZEL-LEZ-HAMEAU	6th	9 a.m.	Officers & N.C.Os proceeded to take part in tactical scheme under Lt Col CHEYNE in vicinity of POMMERA. O.C. remained in camp for purpose of making sanitary & other arrangements in new billets	
"		12 noon	Lieut H.A. ROBERTSON returned from 14th Divl Grenade School.	
"	7th	3.30 p.m.	Church Parade.	
"	8th	6.30 p.m.	Officers & N.C.Os & men proceeded to MANIN for night operations	
"	9th	11 a.m.	Officers & N.C.Os men proceeded to MANIN for tactical scheme under Lt Col CHEYNE.	
"	10th	9 a.m.	3 6 Bombers proceeded to Divl Grenade School to assist in demonstration before Army & Corps Staff returning at 6 p.m.	

Army Form C. 2118.

WAR DIARY
or
INTELLIGENCE SUMMARY

(Erase heading not required.)

Place	Date	Hour	Summary of Events and Information	Remarks and references to Appendices
IZEL-LEZ-HAMEAU	May 11	9 am	Officers to H.C. Down proceeded to HAMEAU for tactical scheme under Lt Col CHEYNE	
		12 n	Company moved into new billets at MANIN in order to form 6th Corps Cyclist Batln and this unit then came under the orders of S.O.C. 6th Corps and ceased to be 14th Divl Cyclist Coy. O.C. assumed command of 6th Corps Cyclist Battalion	

121/7935

14th Divisional Cyclist Coy.

Nominal Roll of Officers & men proceeding with this Unit.

Number	Rank & Name	Where employed
	Capt. M. A. Fowler.	
	Lieut H. D. Harrison	
	" S. R. K. Gunner.	Hut Construction Camp
	" H. A. Robertson	
	" A. L. Mare.	O/c Platoon at 14th Div Hd. Qtrs.
	" S. Shepherd.	O/c Road Controls.
	2/Lieut A. L. Williams	Hut Construction Camp
	" R. F. Gwyn.	
5314	Coy Sgt Major T. J. Mitchell	
3258	Coy Qtr Mtr Sgt W. H. Wyke.	
3931	Sgt D. Robertson	
3269	" A. F. Harris	
3911	" C. Bowers.	
4987	" E. Dyer.	Town Major Poperinghe
3302	" J. Shaw.	
4160	" G. H. Phillips	14th Divl. Hq. Qtrs.
3255	" R. F. Wolsey.	
3270	L/Sgt. E. J. Mercy.	
5165	" C. Allton	
3970	" F. Coe.	A.P.M. 14th Div.
5249	" W. H. Fowler.	
3271	Corpl. W. Congdon.	14th Div Hd. Qtrs.
3926	" F. Garside	on Leave.
3969	" J. Molloy.	14th Div Hd Qtrs.
5052	" F. W. Reed	
3904	" A Ryder	on leave
3259	" C. H. Shock.	

14th Divisional Cyclist Coy.

Number.	Rank & Name.	Where employed.
2733.	Corpl. S. Smith	
3956.	" O. Wilcox	
5157	L/Cpl. F. W. Blunt.	A. P. M. 14th Div.
5170	" C. Cox	do.
3257	" F. Dolman	Town Major Poperinghe
5143.	" H. Frettingham	
2726	" G. Haines	A. P. M. 14th Div.
4988	" E. Hopton	14th Div Hd. Qts.
5295	" L. Horseman	
2727	" E. Haskins	
3930	" L. Levy.	
5312	" W. Munford.	
2724	" G. C. Martin.	
3266.	" A. H. Parsons	
2721.	" J. Pritchard	On leave.
5319	" S. Skelcher.	14th Div Hd. Qts.
3896	" C. J. Streeter	
4985	" W. Skelly.	A. P. M. 14th Div.
3656	" J. Leggett.	
3276.	" W. T. Smith	
3273	" J. Saunders.	
3952.	" P. W. Toms.	
3933	" A. E. Tetlow	
5055	" A. Taylor.	
3914	" W. Worman.	
5301.	" J. T. Walvin	
3927	Pte. W. Ashton.	
2855	" G. Appleyard.	
5306	" E. Ayres.	14th Div Hd. Qts.
2846	" G. Angus.	do

14th Divisional Cyclist Coy.
─────────

Number.	Rank & Name.	Where Employed.
5308.	Pte H. Beckinsale	
5307	" A. Belson.	14th Hd. Qtrs.
3657	" J. Boys.	
4169.	" F. Copeland.	14th Divl. Signal Coy.
5166.	" R. Bradshaw.	14th Hd. Qtrs.
5164	" J. Boddington	14th Divl Signal Coy.
5140	" A. Beards.	
3557	" J. Baynam.	14th Divl. Signal Coy.
5159	" H. Bennett.	do.
5154	" A. H. Barton	14th Hd. Qtrs.
3260	" L. Banks.	
5325	" J. Benson	Rest area Signals
5289	" T. Butler	
5324	" A. J. Barnes.	
3902	" W. Beetison	Road Controls
3939	" E. Bartlett.	
3940	" C. Broad	
3907	" T. Blake	
671	" G. Ballinger	
5334	" G. Cartwright	
3900	" J. Cole.	
2180	" J. Clayton.	
3161.	" W. Clayton.	
5167	" A. J. Chinnery	14th Divl Signal Coy.
7218	" B. A. Cooper.	14th Hd. Qtrs.
6457	" J. Coe.	
3903	" H. Cook.	Town Major. Poperinghe
3653	" M. Cooke.	
4501	" J. W. Cooke.	Road Controls.
3963	" H. Charlette.	

14th Divisional Cyclist Coy.

Number	Rank & Name	Where employed
4979	Pte W. Chapple.	14th Divl Hd Qtrs.
5309	" A. Cusworth.	do.
4975	" J. Dennis	
5310	" E. J. Davies	Road Controls
7032	" S. Davidson	
3262	" L. A. Davis	14th Divl Hd Qtrs.
3290	" W. Dakers.	
3651	" W. H Daniel	
4977	" F. Down.	Road Control.
3649	" J. Davis	
7995	" S. Durose.	14th Divl Hd Qtrs.
3550	" B. Denny.	Road Control.
7879	" A. Davis	
2729	" A. F. Dinham	
99	" A. Drunk.	
3921	" A. Dibbs	
3908	" H. Druber.	Road Control
3944	" H. Dennis	14th Divl Signal Coy.
3925	" C. Elliott	
7407	" J. Edwards.	
7272	" F. Evans.	
2732	" H East	Road Control
5144	" H. Fitzgerald.	14th Div. Hd Qtrs.
3929	" J. Gilmore	
3919	" W. Gurmin	Rest area Signals
134	" J. Gouge.	
4989	" W. Garland	
3972	" W. Goodway.	
4972	" A. Hearn	14th Divl Hd Qtrs
3652	" S. Higgins	

14th Divisional Cyclist Coy.

Number.	Rank & Name.	Where Employed.
5050.	Pte A. Hardy.	
3265	" E. Horton	
1845	" J. Hannigan	
5175	" F. Hipkiss	Road Control
5142	" E. Harrison	14th Divl Police
3264	" C. D. Hall.	Road Control
5292	" A. Husbands	do.
5341.	" J. W. Hill	do.
3901.	" W. H Hobbs.	
3958	" B. Hawksworth.	
4508	" W. Harris	
3954	" W. Hudson	Road Control
2714	" S. Isaacs.	14th Divl Hd Qtrs.
3968	" J. Jones.	
3647	" E. Jenkins	
2887	" A. Janks.	14th Div. Hd Qtrs.
4471.	" A. Jeffery.	
5343	" A. Jones.	
5296	" J. Johnson.	
5169	" W. J. Knight	14th Divl Hd Qtrs.
5311.	" G. Knipe	14th Divl Hd Qtrs.
3275	" A. E. Lewis	
3630	" G. Leech.	
2725	" G. Leonard.	
5298	" W. Moran.	
3898	" L. Morris	
5299	" W. McAree.	
3915	" W. Murray.	Road Control
5297	" H. Milne	
2723	" B. Mills	

14th Divisional Cyclist Coy.

Number.	Rank & Name.	Where employed.
5332.	Pte. R. Magness.	
2715	" H. Munch.	14th Div. Hd. Qters.
3928	" J. Norman.	
5333	" H. Owen.	
3912.	" J. Oakes.	14th Div. Hd. Qters.
5315	" S. Penn.	14th Div. Police.
5145.	" F. Pyett.	14th Div. Hd. Qters.
3268	" L. Plantmason	
3946	" E. Potter.	
5337	" L. Phillips	
5342.	" T. W. Parry.	
5300.	" E. Raper.	
5152	" A. Read.	14th Divl Signal Coy.
5316	" F. Robson.	
4166.	" T. Sowerby.	
5317	" E. Slough.	14th Divl Police
2718	" S. Skiller	14th Divl Hd. Qters.
5318.	" W. Slyvester.	
3951.	" R. Stott.	
3648	" E. Spence.	
3655	" J. Sanderson.	
5150.	" A. Shale.	
3553	" W. Snell.	14th Div. Signal Coy.
7046	" F. J. Salisbury	
3938	" S. Singer	
3910	" G. Scott.	
3953	" B. E. Stacey.	
3936.	" E. Smith	
3897.	" W. C. Tasker.	
5156	" G. Thorne.	Road Controls

14th Divisional Cyclist Coy.

Number.	Rank & Name.	Where Employed
3555.	Pte H. Taylor.	14th Divl Police.
906.	" D. Thomas.	14th Divl. Hd Qters.
3654	" W. Taylor.	
4010	" F. C. Tucker.	
5320	" W. Thorne.	14th Divl. Hd Qters.
5177	" W. Thorogood.	do.
3554	" G. Waine	
5141.	" C. Wheeler.	
5168	" R. Worden.	14th Divl Police
5340	" A. Walker.	
5323	" W. Wilde	
5302	" R. Wood.	
3274	" C. Wyles.	
3941.	" J. H. Wilson	
3947	" G. Wilson	
5303	" J. D. Wilson	
5305	" J. Wilson	
5304	" A. Wakenshaw.	14th Divl Police
5330	" F. Wright	
3937	" W. Whitnell	
3559.	" A. B. Whitham	
5522.	" G. Young.	

Fowler
Capt.
COMMANDING
14TH DIVISIONAL CYCLIST COMPANY.

www.ingramcontent.com/pod-product-compliance
Lightning Source LLC
Chambersburg PA
CBHW081439160426
43193CB00013B/2326